WOMEN RISING

REAL WOMEN EMBRACING CHANGE AND TRANSFORMATION

CHANTELLE ADAMS

STOKE PUBLISHING

Editor: Joanna Bell
Published by STOKE Publishing

ISBN: 978-1-988675-40-4
Self-Help/Women's Studies

CONTENTS

INTRODUCTION

CHANTELLE ADAMS

There are times in our life when we feel crushed under the weight of the world's expectations… when we feel like the world is crumbling around us, out of our control… when the pain and loss is so great that we struggle to breathe. Our soul is suffocating and crying out for us to set it free.

In that moment we have a choice.

A choice to remain silent in our suffering – or a choice to create life anew.

These choices we make determine our reality. It is up to us to decide.

But deciding can be the most difficult part, because our hearts can be telling us one thing, while our minds conjure up all kinds of fears, doubts and what ifs.

In that moment of fear, what we are called to do is listen.

Listen to the truth and wisdom within.

Listen to what our soul is calling for us to do.

Listen.

And then act from that place within us, where we hold all the answers we seek.

The women in this compilation have all been at a crossroads in their life and have chosen their path outside of the fears, doubts and what ifs… outside of the pain and struggle. They chose truth – and then they put one foot in front of the other and walked that path, no matter how hard it was at the time.

When we trust the path, even when we can't see the end of the road, we are leaning into our faith and a higher power. This act of faith can and will guide us on this journey, but we must take that first step ourselves, towards our new way of being.

It is from our greatest struggles in life that we learn the greatest lessons. From those lessons, we become our greatest self.

And it is through sharing the struggle, heartache, loss, pain, grief – and the truth, love, peace and joy on the other side – that we know we are not alone on this journey called life. You are not alone in your pain.

You are not alone in the hardships you face.

You are not alone in the messiness of life.

You are not alone.

Sharing your story, all the real and raw bits of it, can be incredibly scary, but also incredibly freeing… as the authors of so many of the stories within the pages of this book found out. You will read some that will feel like a reflection of your own path and others that will not, but the essence of their messages will speak to your soul and begin a stirring within.

I believe you are reading this book for a reason. It found its way to you because there is a message your heart needs to hear – and you are ready to listen.

You are ready to let go, forgive, love deeper, see the beauty in the struggle and choose.

Choose you.

Choose a new way of living and leading.

Choose to let go and forgive.

Choose to leave a legacy for a loved one you have lost.

Choose to create.

Choose to believe you are worthy and you matter.

Choose to trust the unfolding.

Choose to be happy, no matter what.

The choice is yours.

And we are here cheering you on. As you read and take action, you will begin to see that this book is giving you permission to take imperfect action, to defy the odds, to go against the "shoulds," to start over, to heal, to take that next right step…

Ultimately this book is giving you permission to RISE UP.

Rise up above the hate, the pain, the feelings of defeat – and embrace the love, the truth and the new way of living your life – fully expressed and fully alive.

Be open and listen as you read each story and when you feel the soul shivers, take note. Then, take courageous action, because there lies the catalyst for change.

You are standing at a crossroads in your life. Change is on the horizon.

Just remember, you have the power within you to create your own reality. All you need to do is decide.

Take a few deep breaths, let go of the past, open your heart to what is possible – and let these stories stir within you and awaken the truth that has always been there.

Because together we can and will rise.

xo Chantelle Adams

www.chantelleadams.com

FLOURISH FEARLESSLY

"Trust that the world will not stop spinning when you take a moment for yourself. When you release the guilt of making yourself a priority – to slow down, to heal – that is where you will truly flourish."
– Annette Stephenson

I am a strong woman; I come from a place where women are strong, but there was a time when I was not strong. This is my story.

In 2007, on my small island of Grand Cayman, I was leading the charge as a pioneer in the healthcare industry by starting the first ever audiology clinic. Here I was, a local girl, who by many standards should not have even thought about entering into this arena, but I was doing it anyway. After many years of blood, sweat and tears, I found myself in a place of success. I was able to control the outcomes in this space and get exactly what I wanted. I was going for it all, expanding my team and services. Then in December 2016, I got a little surprise. I was pregnant! Now, being pregnant and having a child was the furthest thing from my mind at the time and was not written in my five-year plan. But here I was, pregnant for the first time, at thirty-eight.

To say I was in shock is an understatement! Not only was I questioning if I could be a good mom, but I was wondering, *How is this going to work with my business and my life as an entrepreneur? Am I going to be able to balance these worlds?*

Then we received an even bigger surprise. During a routine ultrasound, two weeks after finding out I was pregnant, my doctor found not one, not two, but three heartbeats!!Triplets!!! Three beautiful babies were coming to me, for me to be their mom.

It took me some time to adjust to the idea of this new plan, this new way of being and living. This place where I had to release control because I no longer had control over everything and didn't know exactly what was going to happen. But I carried on as usual, following my path of working hard and showing up every single day, even though it was a lot to carry. Literally a lot to carry, with three babies inside me!

I had been flying out to a doctor in Miami for checkups because the island doesn't have all of the equipment necessary for this type of high-risk pregnancy. In fact, we were making plans to relocate to Miami for the last few weeks of the pregnancy. We planned to remain there to have the babies, and to stay afterwards for whatever length of time necessary until we could safely fly back home to Cayman.

On April 11, 2017, I was twenty-two weeks along and preparing to leave for Miami for a final check-up. My water broke. In that moment fear washed over me. I felt it so powerfully coursing through my veins, the fear of what I knew was going to happen to my babies. Here I was again – someone who loved to understand what was happening and have a plan, and I had to step into a place of needing to trust and let go of control. But even in that moment, I was not able to fully release control – instead of being open to receive, I was still trying to maintain control during the worst time of my life.

Within twenty-four hours of my water breaking, I delivered Tianna, who was born sleeping. Her identical sister Isabella, and then their fraternal sister Emma followed. They both lived for a few minutes before they joined their sister in heaven. This loss was excruciating to bear.

After this significant loss, I chose to give myself the space I needed to heal. During this healing process, I realized that there was a lot I needed to learn and a lot that my precious baby girls came to teach me. I had spent so much of my life doing for others. I was living a life dictated by others, and not listening to the desires of my heart, not trusting myself and most of all, not making myself a priority. Even during pregnancy, I was running around doing everything for everyone and not making myself or my babies the priority because I just thought everything would be fine and I could keep doing all the things I had always done. So as a last final attempt to get my attention, God and my babies decided that I had to be shaken to my core to wake up and realize that I needed to step up and start living in my truth.

Here I am, on the other side of what was undeniably the worst time of my life and entering what may be the best time of my life so far. I took the time I needed to heal and as a result, things in my life have flourished. My business has grown, relationships that matter to me are enhanced, and most of all, I have thrived. I've started to trust my intuition more. I have started doing more of the things that matter to me without feeling guilty or feeling the need to ask anyone for permission to live my life. I am beginning to live life on my terms.

I don't want you to feel sorry for me. I'm not sharing my story for pity. I'm sharing the story of my three beautiful daughters to honour them. I am called to share my story because I know the message I have to share is so powerful – *that we as women are here to do big things* – to create change, to stand up, to speak up and to have our voices heard. But we also need to release control of the outcome, release the need to have it all planned out because there could be a more significant plan unfolding than we can even imagine.

Maybe you've also experienced the loss of a pregnancy or the loss of a child. Perhaps you have lost yourself and are going through life people-pleasing and denying yourself your desires and happiness. If you are an entrepreneur, maybe you have had a time where you didn't feel good enough, or had a moment of failure in your business and now you need to heal.

For just a moment, I want you to let go of those thoughts and be right here with me, right now. Most of all, stop doing what others expect of you and do what matters most to you. Trust that the world will not stop spinning when you take a moment for yourself. When you release the guilt of making yourself a priority – to slow down, to heal – that is where you will truly flourish.

Time to stop asking others for permission to live your life. Do not feel guilty for making yourself a priority. We only have one life to live! This is not a dress rehearsal, and you have to make the most out of this life. Don't wake up one morning and look back and have regrets for all of the things that you did not do, because you were made to feel guilty for wanting to follow your dreams.

As you step out with courage – letting go of the fear of judgment, the fear of rejection, the fear of failure, the fear of success – step fully into what you claim as truly yours in your life, your business and for your family. When you no longer settle for someone else's standards, that is where the shift will happen.

That is when you will flourish fearlessly!

Rise Up Challenge

1. Do one thing that you deeply desire to do but haven't done yet because you don't feel you deserve it.
2. Take five minutes every day to just be still. No phone, no distractions. Just you in the peace and quiet.
3. Cultivate what matters to you and not what is expected.

About the Author

Dr. Annette Stephenson is a board certified audiologist with a private practice clinic in the Cayman Islands. She has the only audiology clinic on the island and has been open for over a decade.

Outside of audiology, Annette is also fiercely committed to guiding women who feel guilty for doing what matters to them instead of doing what is expected. She has years of experience working with clients who have had similar worries and concerns as these and uses her personal story to guide them to achieve remarkable success. Her mission is for women to hear their truth – to own the fact that saying yes to themselves doesn't mean that life will stop, and to be empowered to make themselves a priority. What lights her up about her work is knowing that she can provide the gift of healing and compassion to women who are at any stage of an uncertain situation, struggling to find a solution so that they can flourish fearlessly.

In addition to being an advocate for self-care, Annette is also starting a foundation to champion for those whose lives have been affected by the heartbreaking loss of a baby through pregnancy loss or stillbirth. The foundation will fund research and development in improving maternal and neonatal healthcare on her home island of Grand Cayman.

Find out more about Annette's work at www.annettestephenson.com.

2

LOVE IS THE CURE

THE SELF-LOVE FORMULA FOR CREATING A LIFE
THAT HONOURS YOUR HEART!

"The discovery that we are all fully capable, right now, of inspiring change and moving others to act through collective courage, was a game changer for me. Teaching women how to practice self-love is a soul fulfilling journey. Together we can heal ourselves and the world."
– Janna Hare

Myth#1: Love is easy, effortless and offers eternal happiness.

Fact: Love takes courage, time, effort and attention.

Myth #2: Self-love is selfish.

Fact: Self-love is an act of honour and self-respect.

Myth #3: People who love themselves are self-centered.

Fact: Self-love attracts choosing what is good for you and respecting that others have their own free will.

We live in a society that romanticizes the notion of love. Many of us believe that our worthiness comes from how much we love **other** people in our lives. Or, we believe that our happiness is dependent on other people making us happy! Love is so much more than what we witnessed or were taught growing up. We were rarely, if ever, taught the concept of self-love.

How many of you can remember being in a place of feeling you were "not enough?" Of not loving yourself?

Not skinny enough? Not attractive enough? Not smart enough? Not athletic enough? Not ambitious enough? Not _____ (fill in the blank) enough?

Never enough. Ugh.

Well, I don't know about you, but I remember being in this place of "not enough-ness" for too many years! I had climbed to a wonderful level of success in my career. I had a seat around an executive table and there were many great things going on in my life. From the outside looking in, people would see success, drive and purpose. They would say, "Look at her doing BIG things!" Yes, I was a leader. Yet at the *same time,* I felt I was never quite enough.

I lived in a flurry of activity, achievement and success, yet I felt like I could never measure up. I suffered chronically from this "not enough" affliction. It was running a negative-feedback-loop in my head. "I am not skinny enough. I am not attractive enough. I am not smart enough. I am not rich enough." Never enough. Sheesh!

I vividly remember my face-down moment. I was away on an amazing trip with my husband. In theory, the trip was to enjoy each other's company. In practice, I found myself projecting my "not enough-ness" onto him. I made remarks that triggered an epic fight. Who can relate to this? So here I was, drowning in this deep sea of truly not loving myself. I projected my "not enough-ness" onto the man I love. How often do we do this in life, relationships and business? Far too often. Lack of self-love is a global epidemic that prevents us from having meaningful relationships with ourselves – and ultimately, with everyone else we care about.

When I got home from my trip, I called up one of my coaching friends. I shared with her that I was sick and tired of beating myself up. I could not keep up with all the demands I had placed on myself. I was: trashing myself, mad at myself, feeling like crap and saying things that I would never dream of saying to someone else – all as a result of not being able to keep up with everything. Out of all the wisdom my friend shared with me, I most remember her asking if she could do an *exercise* with me. Well, S-H-T-F (shit hit the fan)! D'oh!

It was that exercise that changed my life. Without getting into all the gory details, I learned from the experience *exactly* how negative I was towards myself. Using my two-year-old grandson as the main character in the exercise, it became crystal clear that my self-talk was gag worthy! I said things to myself that I would NEVER say to another human being.

I realized then and there that I needed to get curious. I know it's not just me that has this struggle. From this curiosity, a formula for self-love was developed. After extensive validation through teaching and testing, I learned that self-love begins with self-care and self-compassion. Your level of self-love is either damaged or amplified by your self-talk. So, the formula is this:

Self-talk x (Self-care + Self-compassion) = Self-love.

Your self-talk is the messenger that choreographs your life, actions and results.

If we look at our self-talk, we can see that our stories – what we make up about ourselves – are what we become!

Whooooahhhhhhh.

So, I bet you're wondering now – how the heck do we shift negative self-talk?

Good question! That was exactly what I wondered too. After much research, the Freedom Queue (FQ) process was born. We developed this process to help clear away all the false stories you tell yourself. It can help the shift from negative self-talk to positive self-talk.

Here is what the FQ process looks like:

Step 1: Think about the stories you tell yourself.

Step 2: Get clear on the way you speak to yourself.

Step 3: THIS IS THE MOST IMPORTANT STEP!

"Cancel" or "FQ" the negative self-talk. Next, immediately say something kind to yourself – for example, "Gosh! My hair looks good today!"

Step 4: Get curious! Journal about the truth behind this negative self-talk. You can begin to SHIFT the stories with new narratives about yourself. Write the story with a positive focus.

Step 5: Ask yourself the five Rise Up questions that are at the end of this chapter. These questions will help you breathe positive energy into your "ONE BIG BEAUTIFUL LIFE!"

After following steps one through five, you're now ready to start paying attention to the next part of our formula – self-care.

This is my invitation to you today: give yourself permission to take care of yourself. Put yourself on your to-do list. Carve out space in your day to fill yourself up first. Get clear on your self-care goals. Be intentional. Now, ACT with commitment!

You see, any intention you set without commitment, goes nowhere. When things go awry, remember you need to stay committed: to your goals, to yourself and to your self-care. Not honouring a commitment to yourself is a form of self-betrayal! You activate massive self-trust when you keep your commitments to yourself. Then, your actions will align with the results you want!

If you find yourself lacking self-trust, or even in a space of self-betrayal, you must *lean in* to self-compassion. To learn to trust yourself again, you must lead with compassion. Sure, we will mess up – but if we can practice self-compassion, we can learn to forgive ourselves for our mistakes.

As we discover the richness that positive self-talk gives us, and develop healthy self-care and self-compassion practices, we ultimately find ourselves in a place of love. When we release self-judgment, shame, guilt and comparison, we give ourselves permission to rise – because we are free from all the baggage that weighs us down.

I invite (and challenge) you to stop circling the drain. I want you to call bullshit on the messages you send to yourself that are keeping you small. It is not easy work, but positive self-care, self-compassion and self-talk practices are the ingredients that lead to *massive* self-love. Together we can heal ourselves, and collectively make a bigger impact, because what I know for sure is that LOVE IS THE CURE!

Rise Up Challenge

Who are you when you're being you?

Capture the answers to these questions in your journal:

1. What are you doing when you are experiencing the greatest joy, happiness and fulfillment?
2. What are you thinking when you're in this place?
3. What does it feel like to be this person?
4. What are you saying to yourself, about yourself, when you're being this person?
5. How are you treating yourself when you're being this person?

Now, the million-dollar question: how many hours in a week are you truly being this person? How many would you like it to be? What are the practices that can help you create a life that honours your heart? What support do you need?

About the Author

Janna Hare, Self-love Catalyst, Authenticity Advocate, Bullshit Fighter As an accredited coach, educator and transformational leader, Janna leverages her finely tuned insight and ability to understand and connect with people to support them on their journeys. Her work as co-founder of Leaderista Inc. is all about helping women break through glass ceilings and create new paradigms that support who they truly want to be in the world.

Janna is passionate about and committed to helping women release their self-imposed limitations and embrace the integrity of fully being themselves. She is also the CEO and founder of Spark Leadership Inc.

Learn more about Janna's work at www.leaderista.com and www.sparkleadership.ca.

3

LITTLE VOICE, BIG BUSINESS

HOW TO KICK FEAR IN THE FACE AND GO BIG EVEN IF YOU'RE SCARED AS HELL

"If it makes you feel like throwing up, it's a good sign."
– Nadia Finer

I remember the first time I realized there was something a bit odd about my voice. I was fifteen, in a French lesson, and we'd just got these fancy new tape machines. You spoke into the headset and recorded your voice onto the tape so you could listen to yourself and check your pronunciation. I loved French, despite my appalling British accent. So I happily recorded myself, then pressed play.

All I could hear was this little kid talking. Who the heck was that?

It took me a moment to understand that it was me.

I was mortified.

From that day on, I vowed to keep this little voice of mine under wraps. I shrunk, determined to be as inconspicuous as I could, afraid that people would judge me or laugh at me.

Yes, I could probably run some kind of dodgy phone sex line if I was ever particularly strapped for cash; the guys at the local Thai take-away always know it's me when I ring up; I get what I want when I complain about something and, of course, I'm truly excellent at swearing – bloody brilliant, in fact. But while I might sound like I was born to do cartoon voice-over work, my voice has always made me feel insecure – like people wouldn't take me seriously.

This is hardly surprising – roughly once a week, someone will call our house – and when they hear my voice, they get confused, take an uncomfortably long pause, and then ask to speak to my mom.

I am the mom!

And of course, when I started as an entrepreneur, it was a bit of a problem.

My preferred working position was hidden away behind my laptop. Given the chance, I avoided speaking on the phone. Leaving voice messages struck me as complete madness when a text would do. I'd give all forms of photography and video an extremely wide berth. And public speaking? No, thank you very much.

My constant crisis of confidence even caused me to enter into a business partnership with someone bigger, brasher and ballsier than me so that I could hide in the background.

Although the business looked big and successful on the outside, I was stressed out to the max, unable to sleep and constantly on edge.

One day things came to a head.

My partner and I were talking on the phone when she started to lay into me. "You're playing small. You're holding us back!" I couldn't believe what I was hearing. The aggression in her voice was ugly. I could see her eyes bulging, veins throbbing, spit flying through the air, even over the phone.

My head was spinning. This was the business I had started on my own. My business. My idea. I was pacing up and down my kitchen in pajamas and slippers, palms sweating as I listened to this tirade of abuse. I could feel everything I'd worked for come crumbling down around me.

"Nobody takes you seriously. You're a joke. You don't deserve to get paid the same as me," she said. I felt a molten volcano of rage rise up within me.

I cleared my throat, took a breath and a steely voice I didn't recognize said, "It's over. You can expect to hear from my lawyer."

I put down the phone, hands shaking, and started to cry. What really bothered me wasn't the shouting. It was the thought that she might be right. What if I really was thinking small? A small-time player with small ambitions and smaller talent? This was the fear that had haunted me all my life.

After a few weeks of wallowing in ice cream on the sofa, I felt a glimmer of strength inside me. I knew that I didn't need her. I knew I could start again. On my own. I'd done it before and I could do it again. But this time it would be different. There would be no more pretending to be someone I wasn't. I was going to do things my way. I was going to put myself at the heart of my business. And I was going to go big. In my own way.

I was ready to break free from fakery and kick fear in the face.

But how real was I prepared to be? Would I have the courage to really face up to the thing that made me, me?

Why on earth would I mention, let alone embrace, my biggest insecurity – the thing that made me feel so uncomfortable? People would never take me seriously. They'd probably even laugh in my face. I just couldn't do it.

I took a deep breath and was reminded of a quote by Joseph Campbell: "The cave you fear to enter holds the treasure you seek." My little voice was my cave. My thing. The very idea of being open about it terrified me. But somehow, I knew it held the key to everything. I got goosebumps just thinking about it. And it turns out, if it gives you goosebumps and makes you want to throw up, it's a good sign!

It was a risk. But I had to at least give it a go. Because the chances are, if I felt little – then so did a lot of my clients. I closed my eyes and decided to take the leap.

That night, as I lay in bed, it came to me. "Little Voice. Big Business." That would be my brand.

And you know what? Since I finally decided to be myself in my business and embrace the thing that makes me unique, I haven't looked back. I may not be a multi-millionaire, a celebrity or a business legend (yet) but what I have done is create a business that allows me to work to scale. It's little, but it gets big results.

I've stopped hiding. I'm out there. In the big wide world. My people love my vulnerability. They love the fact that I share from this raw, real place. It attracted people who became my tribe, my super fans... because I was willing to show up and build a big reputation online.

I stopped looking locally and started thinking globally. I focused like a laser beam on my ideal clients, no matter where they lived in the world.

I raised my prices... significantly. I said goodbye to selling my time for money. I created products I could make money on without lifting a finger.

But I still stayed true to my goals; I didn't let my business get out of control. I didn't splash out on offices or start selling off equity. It was still just me – no complications, no investors, no pesky partners, expensive premises or employees. My business is a serene, lean, money-making machine!

When fear and doubt and limiting beliefs have your business dreams in a headlock, it's so tempting to compare yourself to others and hide yourself away.

If you truly want to grow your business... if you're ready to pump up your profits... if you're ready to go global in your pajamas... if you're ready to embrace that part of you that truly is your gift... you need to let go of your fears. You need to go all in.

It's time to unleash the BIGness in your business.

Rise Up Challenge

1. What's your unique gift? Embrace that unique thing about you! That thing you're hiding is probably the most important thing, the thing you need to shine a light on. No more seeing it as a negative. No more trying to hide it. It's your gift, your uniqueness and it's time to unleash it on the world. Create an unforgettable personal brand. Attract your kind of people.
2. Scale your business in a way that works for you, so you can work less and make more money. Move away from selling time for money and package up your services. Create recurring streams of revenue. Review your prices to ensure you're charging your worth. Automate elements of your business so you're not wasting time doing everything yourself.
3. Think Global. Move from thinking locally to thinking globally, and imagine the possibilities! No more feeling tied to the people who happen to live down the road from you. Focus in on clients who are perfect for you – people who love what you do, that you love to work with, and who are happy to invest in you – no matter where they might live in the world. Build a global brand around who you are and watch your baby grow! Create that big impact you're meant to create in the world.

About the Author

Nadia Finer is a powerhouse business coach, wickedly funny international speaker and author of *Little Me Big Business*.

She has helped hundreds of business owners all over the world to pump up their profits through her Profit Pack business academy and Coachica business coaching helpline.

Don't be fooled by Nadia's sweet appearance and adorable voice. She is feisty and fearless and has learned to embrace her little voice rather than hide behind her insecurities. She turned it into her secret weapon and used it to build a unique personal brand. She now helps struggling business owners all over the world to stop playing small and unleash the BIGness in their business. If you would like to download Nadia's free Strategy Six Pack, dive into her new book, *Little Me BIG Business* or chat with her about business coaching, head over to www.nadiafiner.com.

4

_____

THERE IS PURPOSE IN THE PAIN

HOW IMMENSE GRIEF WAS TURNED INTO PURPOSE

"We are all put on this earth for a reason. We aren't meant to live in darkness and pain forever. We must all know that there is goodness in the darkest and it's okay to shine the light in on it. When we do that, we own the power of turning our mess into our message."
– Karly Wood Kelly

As a little girl, I grew up in Saudi Arabia. I looked totally different from everyone around me. Blonde hair, blue eyes, with an American accent! I was definitely the minority, but I never felt different. I was never bullied or teased. I always felt accepted. No matter how different I looked, I was accepted for who I was.

Eight years later, we moved back to the United States. I was in sixth grade and I remember being nervous for the first time. I have scoliosis and my parents decided it was a good idea to perm

23

my short bowl-like haircut. Picture this – I had to wear a back brace on the OUTSIDE of my clothes, I had a bowl cut, permed hair and I had no clue what was "hip" in the United States. I then went through many years of being bullied and not being accepted. Kids would play the drums on my back with their pencils. In addition to this, little did I know my world was about to be turned upside down yet again.

My parents divorced. I remember as a young girl being shaken up by that moment of change in my life – change that felt out of my control. I didn't understand how to deal with all of these emotions and difficulties that were swirling in my heart and in my mind. This led me down a road of self-harm. I developed an eating disorder that lasted fifteen years. I battled with cutting myself and at age fourteen, I even attempted to take my own life. It was a complicated time in my life. It was messy.

Thankfully, by the grace of God, we moved again. I started high school in a new town. It was there I met Brady. She was my best best friend, my soul sister and literally just my person. She was someone who just got me. We could finish each other's sentences. We had so much fun together – we spent all our time together, then went on to make the best of memories living together in college after high school. She accepted me and all my imperfections. She loved me regardless of mistakes I'd made, and she forgave me for things I said or did.

My life forever changed July 5th, 2010. Brady and I had plans to go out boating for the holiday weekend and for some reason I decided to flip a coin. I flipped a coin to make the choice. Heads, I would go, tails, I would stay. That coin flipped in the air and landed on the back of my hand. I looked at it – it was tails. So, I made the choice to stay home, when I could have very easily gone. That night I was woken up by a phone call and heard the news that completely rocked my world. There had been a boating accident and my best friend was killed.

I can't put into words what this did to my soul – however, I will try. My life flipped upside down. I spiraled back into the dark place I experienced as a fourteen-year-old girl. I didn't know how to deal with the pain I found myself in. The heartache, stress, loss, grief and pain – it was all too much to deal with. I battled with drinking too much and taking too much medication for my back. It was the only thing I could do to numb the pain and my emotions. I didn't have the tools to deal with survivor's guilt, grief, immense heartache and loss. I felt helpless and I began to have bouts of depression and anxiety. It got so bad that I started to isolate myself. I was so afraid of losing others in my life. Being alone felt easier than being surrounded with love. I didn't think I deserved love. At the time, all I could think was, *It should have been me who died and not my best friend.* I was a lost soul for about four years.

Then it all changed. I remember swinging on the porch swing one day. Sunshine was hitting my face and I was feeling its warmth. I smiled. I realized that every day I woke up, I had a choice. Every single day was a new day. Each day was a gift that my dear friend didn't have. I could choose to either continue down the same path – of self-harm, self-destruction, going nowhere, asking myself day in and day out, *What am I doing with my life?* Or, I could take one step at a time, make one choice at a time and truly make something out of this mess that I found myself in. I realized in that moment that I could turn my mess into a message. A message of hope, a message of trust, a message that could lift others out of their own powerful darkness!

I saw what was possible from a place that was still so dark. Remembering the moment where I smiled again shows how simple it can be to make that choice. Something so simple, yet so profound – a smile. That's how dark it had gotten in my life, that a single smile could turn things around.

As I moved forward, I found a community through Beachbody. This community gave me a place to heal. A place to pick up the pieces of my life. It gave me a place to grieve. This supportive team met me where I was at and supported me as I began to work on myself mentally, physically, emotionally and spiritually. I began to truly see the gifts, the lessons and the message in that mess. And I also saw the power in my choices.

It was my choice to turn this mess into a powerful message so I could help others do the same. Our life is a gift and it's meant to be lived to the fullest. I know that there are times in your life when you feel like you cannot go on or the pain is too much to bear. I hope that this story shows that there is another way. You do have a choice and you can turn that pain into something good. There is purpose in everything – it's only when we seek to uncover what it is, that we find the silver lining.

Together we have the power to uplift, inspire and support each other. Many of the lives I have touched have come from sharing my story vulnerably. I am on a mission to continue building a tribe of women who do the same thing – share their mess vulnerably, so they can transform not only their own life, but also the lives around them. We are all put on this earth for a reason. We aren't meant to live in darkness and pain forever. We must all know that there is goodness in the darkest and it's okay to shine the light in on it. When we do that, we own the power of turning our mess into our message.

When we find purpose in our pain, it shines light into our darkness.

Rise Up Challenge

1. Take some time to look back on the tough moments in your life. With each moment, I want you to write down at least one good thing or one lesson or a silver lining that you know came from that experience.
2. What are some new habits you can incorporate into your life? Working out, eating better, meditation, yoga, journaling? Think of things that will create a positive impact in your life.
3. How do you want to feel? Think of the words that represent how you want to feel in your life… for example, sexy, beautiful, grateful or confident. Now think of things you can do that bring you those feelings. Start doing those things daily.

About the Author

Karly's passion for serving women came from a life changing decision to flip a coin about whether to go out on a boat for the weekend with her best friend. The coin decided her fate and she didn't go. That weekend, her friend was killed in an accident on that boat. In working through her grief, she found healing through community support, finding her voice and personal growth. As a result, Karly has become an advocate for women –

helping them to grow, heal and empower themselves.

Karly's work has touched thousands of lives! She is on a mission to help young girls realize that they matter through the initiative she co-founded, GirlSet. She is impacting the lives of women globally by helping them turn their mess into their own message, so they can pay it forward and help other women – creating a massive ripple effect of change in the world.

Karly is married, a fur momma, a motivational speaker and a mindset coach. She is also a certified yoga instructor and is committed to living her best life and paying it forward to others.

Find out more at www.karlykelly.com or email wood.karly@yahoo.com.

5

HAPPINESS CAN BE BOUGHT

SHOWING YOU HOW TIME AND MONEY MATTER
WHEN IT COMES TO HAPPINESS

"I know that we all have the same twenty-four hours in a day. Time is one commodity that you cannot create. When helping my clients use their time more efficiently, so they can focus on what makes them money and be happier in the process, I love to remind them that 'There are seven days in a week and someday isn't one of them.'"
– Jennifer Dunham

"You have cancer."

I felt like I was struck by lightning when I got the news.

That news was the cherry on top of my *bad summer*. I had just turned thirty. I was going through a divorce, hit by a drunk driver and diagnosed with cancer, all within weeks of each other. Someone was trying to get my attention, saying "Wake up, Jennifer!" But it wasn't a dream.

These pivotal, lightning-bolt moments would be life-changing lessons that would illustrate the connection between time, money and happiness – to show me how to fully live – but I wouldn't understand that until much later.

Fast forward a decade.

I remember very clearly a moment when we were living in what my second husband dubbed *suburbia hell*. He was not happy about where we were living – so I was not happy, because he was not happy. Transitive unhappiness.

We found ourselves stuck settling, being okay with just being okay. *So many people live here,* we thought.

We were there, sitting on our deck and having this very serious heart to heart conversation about our future and where we wanted to live when we retire.

"I want some property away from the city," my husband shared.

The neighbour's dogs were barking incessantly in the background.

"What state should we move to?" I asked.

"Shut up!" he yelled at the dogs.

Interruption after interruption. Finally my husband had had enough, stormed back into the house, slammed the door and left me alone with my thoughts.

I wondered: Were we really living our truest happiness?

There are moments in your life when you can settle or choose to pivot.

I knew in my heart, and mind, that I would not settle like that in my life, in my business or in my relationships.

I walked back into that house and announced, "We need to move. Now!" There is no such concept as "retirement" for entrepreneurs. Seven days later, we had found a place just outside the city – acreage with chickens and all.

I know the power in quick decisions and fast action. I know that we all have the same twenty-four hours in a day. Time is one commodity that you cannot create. When helping my clients use their time more efficiently, so they can focus on what makes them money and be happier in the process, I love to remind them that "There are seven days in a week and *someday* isn't one of them."

In seven days we created a massive change in our lifestyle, in our businesses, in our success, in how we showed up for each other and in our relationships. We did it all by making a powerful decision. There is no time for settling and for just okay.

Go big or go home. A mantra that I've always embraced. We took big risks. But once I was able to trade in my high heels for chicken boots on that beautiful farm, the secret I discovered was that the tiniest of habits, done over and over, make the most powerful impact. When you start stacking those habits on top of each other, they create these powerful routines.

We repeat 40% of what we do every single day. Using tiny habits to increase automation by just one more percent can help us get more time in our day, money in the bank and happiness in our lives.

I remember moving onto this farm and completely shifting our lifestyle. I found that as I walked out in my chicken boots and sat with my hot cup of coffee for even just five minutes, it became my *daily grounding point*. The point in my life where I come alive and feel so connected and clear and happy.

Tiny habits help us automate more so we get more time in our day and money in the bank.

We can all benefit from what I call Brain Bliss Activation, where we create connection between our brains and happiness. Increased happiness is known to improve productivity. We can create a different kind of success in business… in our lifestyle. Success without sacrifice. Now I'm not saying this doesn't take work, even hard work at times.

But it all comes back to happiness. People may not agree that money can buy happiness, but they're wrong.

Happiness can be bought!

Entrepreneurs have a tough time being happy if they are struggling with money. There is a huge connection between wealth and happiness. There is a certain level of money we need to survive. Another level to thrive. I see the connection when we attain that income and then we feel more alive. We have less stress and more experiences when we have the income to support the life we desire.

But you must be careful.

Time, Money and Happiness are interconnected… a web… woven together in such a way that you must master all three together. One by itself is not enough.

I had been running my seven figure IT firm for years but found I wasn't fulfilled. So, I also jumped into a creative business, became an award-winning photographer, and soon found myself burnt out, working constantly. I had traded my time for money. Though I loved photography, I was working so hard that I had no time for myself anymore. No time creates a lack of balance.

Time, Money and Happiness are the foundation of how we can truly create the profitable lifestyle and the business that we desire and that we love. I help people create their *Dashes for Cash*, where they create the most income with the least amount of effort, in the least amount of time. I lead them to find the confidence to make an offer, to value what they offer, and to launch it BEFORE they are ready. If they wait to launch WHEN they are ready, many would never launch due to perfectionism and fear. And most importantly, I help them to leverage what is right in front of them – to realize that money actually does grow on trees, you just have to pick the leaves.

So, in my transition, while running my IT business and launching Time, Money and Happiness Matters, I continue to walk my talk. I wear an hourglass necklace to remind me that we all have the same number of hours and it matters what we choose to do with our time.

You can take those high heels and wear them with style. You can change into chicken boots and wear those with style too. You can create a life and a business that lights you up, that you love. And you'll do this when you learn to decide quick, to cherish the life and the time that you have and realize that we all have the same amount of time in the day.

It is time to quit settling, stop being okay with just okay. Choose to stack habits into powerful routines that will save you time

AND increase your income and your happiness. You can create a business that gives you the financial freedom to live your dreams and live each moment.

The biggest shift you can make is to focus and realize that Time, Money and Happiness Matters.

Rise Up Challenge

1. You cannot improve your time, money or happiness if you don't know how you are spending your time right now. Take inventory of how you spend your days. I recommend you write down all of your activities for three to five days in a row.
2. Put smiley faces next to those items that make you happy. Put unhappy faces next to those things you dread. And put $$ next to the activities that directly relate to you making money.
3. Analyze your results. Do you have happy faces every day? Do you have $$ every business day? How many of your unhappy faces can you stop doing? Can you replace those tasks with other ones, delegate them to someone else, postpone them or eliminate them?

About the Author

As a Time, Money and Happiness lifestyle coach, Jennifer helps driven professionals learn how to love their success and career and fully love their lives.

Jennifer's approach is rooted in her IT background. She's a huge believer in automation, habits, repeatable processes and streamlining to reduce overwhelm so you can focus on what matters most. She teaches her clients how to find more time, so they can make more money and increase their happiness.

 Jennifer is a motivational speaker. Audiences love Jennifer's relatable stories and specific strategies that they can use right away to help them grow and scale their business in a way that aligns with their desired lifestyle and values. Jennifer is a cancer survivor. She knows "Life Is Short" and she will tell it to you like it is.

When Jennifer isn't working, you will find her hiking with her hubby, playing with their kitties Zipper and Velcro, or tending to their small chicken farm in the Sierra foothills in Northern California.

If you're ready to expand your business, find More Time, More Money and More Happiness, get Jennifer's Ultimate Habit Bundle at www.happinessmatters.com/UHB-Riseup.

6

SURRENDER TO YOUR MESS

HELPING YOU TO KNOW THAT YOU MATTER AND THAT YOU HAVE THE POWER TO TURN ANY MESS INTO A POWERFUL MESSAGE

"Each mess – be it a moment of loss, pain, struggle or failure in our lives – creates an opportunity for us to learn, for us to grow and for us to find the message in that mess."
– Natasha Hemmingway

In every moment we have a choice. In every mess we have an opportunity to choose to rise up – to choose to live, to choose to share our stories with the world. I want to share my story with you. When I was just two months old, I lost my dad in a car accident. My mom, though, was so strong. It was just me and my mom, but her strength was beautiful to watch and behold.

She found her strength through faith, not fear. She was resilient and continued to push through, no matter what obstacle was put in her way. I remember watching her juggle everything as a single mom and being so strong. Watching how she would rise up each time she would stumble.

When she found herself in a difficult place, she would rise. I knew when I grew up, I wanted to be just like her. She taught me so much. Most importantly, she taught me to keep fighting and to always get back up.

Whenever I saw the strength that was in my mom, it catapulted me into this place of perfection. The strength through loss that we had woven throughout both of our lives took me to this place where I had to overachieve, overanalyze, over control each situation. I felt that if I could plan and control, then I could achieve success – and with success, perhaps I could keep us away from those negative feelings and circumstances.

If I just planned enough, controlled enough, did enough, then we wouldn't have to continue to go through the loss, the pain, the mess. I was always a Type A driven perfectionist from that point forward. I landed a high end job as a medical device sales rep. At one point, I was the only African American woman at that level of position in my industry.

I got married and then divorced. Interestingly, it didn't feel like a failed marriage. It felt like a reminder that I have a choice – that I hadn't been leaning into trusting that guidance that I have within me. That faith. And that I said yes in a moment when I truly knew at my core that it was a no.

But again, each mess – be it a moment of loss, pain, struggle or failure in our lives – creates an opportunity for us to learn, for us to grow and for us to find the message in that mess. The message was to trust and love again, and I did. I found my husband. I fell in love and in this place of love, security and being supported, I soon after became pregnant. We were excited. We were ready.

I remember going into that moment of delivery scared, yet trusting that things would work out. Oh, it was hard. It was really hard because I had chosen to have a natural birth, but it was so worth it.

Well, our beautiful baby boy joined our family on March 13th. But as he came into this world, struggling to breathe, I remember the fear welling up in me as the nurses quickly whisked him away.

I'll never forget, after many tests were run over five days, the doctor telling us that our baby boy had no brain activity, that he would not live much longer.

So, in my deep, deep pain of anguish, fear, sadness and grief, I found myself clinging to my precious boy. Keeping him close to my heart, memorizing the shape of his face, his little toes and fingers. I was holding onto him for as long as I could.

Having to say goodbye forever to the baby boy I longed for, prayed for and cherished, only five days after his birth, crushed me. There is so much pain in losing a child that you have been so desperately waiting to meet. It is a space of devastating heartache and loss.

The guilt, the embarrassment, the feeling that I had failed crept in too.

How could I possibly screw up having a baby?

This is what we are here for. How could I mess that up?

I was struggling. I was grieving. The shame took over. I had to go back to work right away to a stressful sales job.

It was overwhelming to be in this place of grief and having to put on this show that I was okay. 'Cause I couldn't be vulnerable. I couldn't tell people what was really going on. I couldn't allow them in. I had to be strong.

Yet, with all of this swirling around me, at one point I thought, just for a moment, that perhaps it would just be better if I wasn't here on earth. The moment immediately after that thought entered my mind and heart, I knew that I needed to get help. So I did. I put myself into grief counseling.

I remember being in this space of sharing my story and being vulnerable for the first time. I remember finding my strength through my faith and learning that it was okay to be vulnerable. In my culture, we are strong. I started to see that we don't always need to be strong by suffering in silence – that we are better together, and we don't have to do it alone.

I realized that in sharing my story in that safe space, I was no longer hiding. I was able to start to heal because I was giving a voice to that mess and I was finding my message. Through sharing, I also gave others the opportunity to heal and know that they weren't alone.

With this new understanding, I found purpose in my pain. I started to trust and believe again. I leaned all the way into my faith when we got pregnant four months after losing our beautiful boy. It was hard to be grieving, worried and anxious about possibly losing another child. It was hard to be vulnerable, yet it made all the difference.

It was hard to trust and just lean into my faith. I know, without a doubt, no matter where you've been, or what you have been through… no matter the losses, the struggles… no matter the messes that you've found yourself in, you have the power to choose.

There is power in choice. A choice you get to make day after day. A choice that you get to make to not stay stuck, to be open to seeing the lessons, the message and the blessings. The choice to own the mess and to do something good with it.

I am so grateful for both of my beautiful babies. Grateful to be a mom and have my earthly baby in my arms. I'm grateful for the opportunity to step fully into my purpose. To leave that stressful corporate gig and to be supported, not only by my loved ones but also by my faith. I trust that I will be guided and I will be shown the way – and that all I need to do is keep showing up.

Show up for my life and rise up for others. That's what I'm here to help you do. Together we truly can turn our mess into a message. Know that we matter and rise up by finding purpose in our pain.

Rise Up Challenge

1. Own Your Mess: write down one mess that you will own by being vulnerable and transparent.
2. Own Your Choices: write down three things that are not serving you and that you will choose to eliminate.
3. Own Your Message: choose one person or one way you can share your story with someone who may need to hear it and go do it.

About the Author

Natasha helps women move from fear into faith and achieve success on their terms.

Natasha's strength and resilience was fueled after the tragic loss of her newborn son. Her faith was tested further when she found herself juggling the challenges of motherhood with the demands of a highly successful sales career. Her own path of struggle and self-discovery inspires her commitment to helping women and teen girls push past their own pain and fears, and rise into their greatness – so that they too achieve success on their terms.

Natasha helps her clients to lean into their faith, so that they can develop the strength, resilience and confidence they need to achieve success and true joy in their lives. Whether they aspire to start a business, grow their business, get promoted at work, create something beautiful or live to their full potential, Natasha works with her clients to turn their dreams into reality. She has touched hundreds of lives by helping women move from fear into faith and create their reality from a place of truth and trust.

As a sought after motivational speaker, Natasha has spoken internationally on various stages and platforms. She is the cofounder of GirlSet, a self-love initiative to help young girls realize that they matter. When she is not speaking or working with clients, Natasha volunteers at Present Age Ministries to support young girls who have been victims of human sex trafficking. She also speaks on their behalf about prevention, advocacy and awareness in many settings such as schools and community gatherings. She is also happily married and a proud boy mom.

Connect with Natasha at www.natashahemmingway.com and www.girlset.co, and hello@natashahemmingway.com.

7

SHOW YOUR BUSINESS
WHO'S BOSS!

DISCOVER HOW TO MAKE YOUR BUSINESS WORK
FOR YOU

"Business is easy if we'd just get out of our own way."
– Jocelyn Mozak

Have you ever caught yourself asking: "How the hell did I end up here?" Wondering what happened to running *your* business *your* way. Yet, so often it feels like our business is the one running us, instead of us running it.

I'll never forget one night. I'm busy cooking dinner. Carrots are steaming, chicken is in the oven and something's gone sideways on a project from work. Sound familiar?

So, as I'm there trying not to overcook the carrots while simultaneously engrossed in a Skype conversation with my team, in walks my sweet six-year-old son. You know, the one I started this whole business to be a better mom to? Yeah, that one. He comes over wanting to give me a hug and tell me he loves me.

45

Now, do I swoop him up into my arms and receive his love? Nope! Can't he see my sky is falling?!? And with that I shout something about leaving me alone, and can't he see I'm busy. Well, you know what comes next.

Just like that, all the balls that I thought I was so eloquently juggling come crashing to the floor, as my sweet boy goes off in tears. As I slid to the floor, realizing what just happened, I knew in that moment that something had to change.

It was time for me to show my business who was boss!

But how did I get here? Where had I gone wrong?

Before I continue, I want to share just a little bit about my background. I was raised in a home where education and financial security were valued. It never occurred to me that I would do anything else but strive for the best grades, attend the best schools and go after the best jobs.

So that is exactly what I did. I got straight A's, attended Cornell and Stanford University and went to work as an engineer at Intel. By twenty-five, I had it all. I had the job, the house. Heck, I even had the husband. I was excelling at work, doing the things, making the money and I was miserable.

Yet, I felt bound to stay. In my head, leaving would mean being irresponsible and even worse, letting down my gender, my education and my upbringing.

I felt trapped.

Little did I know my children would prove to be my saving grace.

With the birth of my first son I shifted my work schedule to part-time. It seemed like the perfect solution. Yet I quickly found myself feeling like a part-time mom, a part-time employee and a full-time failure. When I was at work I felt like a bad mom, and when I was at home I was a bad employee. I was burning out.

Something had to give. Yet as a mother, I knew that if I was going to let anyone down, it was not going to be my children. So, despite feeling like a failure to my gender, my education and my upbringing, I made the difficult decision to quit...

For I had discovered something far more important to me than following the rules, being responsible and living up to society's expectations.

I had discovered my why.

Well, I quickly learned that while working part-time in corporate was not a solution for me, staying home and bonding with my children 24-7 was not ideal either. I craved community, connection and most importantly, adult conversation.

And so began my entrepreneurial journey. Right from the beginning, my business plan was based around the ages of my kids and the hours of childcare I was comfortable with at each age.

I was creating my business, my way. By having this creative and intellectual outlet I was enabling myself to be a happier person and thus a better mom. My business was meeting my needs and serving my why. It was perfection. At least for a time.

So how exactly did I end up on the floor torn between the carrots, my business and my son?

Simple, with time I lost sight of why.

As my boys got older and began attending school, I started to fall into old patterns of thought. Old stories that said my education and training meant I could and thus *should* be earning more money.

I went from having my business serve me to buying into external definitions of what I thought a business *should* look like. Essentially, I was again buying into someone else's why and I was once again miserable.

It happens to the best of us. We create our business to serve our lives and yet we are human. We can get off track. Thankfully, we can course correct.

So, I want to ask you: why did you start your business?

If you are like most of us, your initial answer probably contained reasons about how you are serving the world and helping others. That's great. But let's dig deeper. How is having a business serving you and your life? What would you need from your business to make it work for you?

If only running a business was as simple as the "work-life balance" cliché – a phrase which I personally hate. To me it conjures up the image of a scale with two clear sides. Work, and everything else. It suggests that the path to perfection is clear – simply divide yourself in two, make sure the two parts are exactly equal and all your problems will be solved.

Well I don't know about you, but my life is not that simple. In fact, my life is quite the opposite. This is the exact reason I began my business in the first place. We are women, mothers, wives, daughters, business owners and so much more. We do not fit into neat boxes.

No, we are amazing beings comprised of many parts that come together to create a whole person and a single life. We must also remember that we are just one person and when our cup is full, it is full.

Your why is the only measuring stick you need to show your business who is boss.

I see too many entrepreneurs who are burnt out, struggling to keep up, drowning in their to-dos and who have completely lost sight of why they started this business in the first place.

Your why matters, and it matters so deeply that you need to hold every decision you make in your life up to it. Only if the project/client/service measures up to your why do you let it in. If it doesn't, you have a choice to make. It either does not belong in your life or you need to find someone else to take care of it because if it does not serve your why, you're not doing it.

We all began our businesses to create a life we love. No, not every day will be perfect. But if your life looks anything like mine did when I was curled up in tears on the kitchen floor, I think it's high time to Show Your Business Who's Boss!

Rise Up Challenge

1. The first step is to remember why you started in the first place. Take a moment to reflect on your why because from this day forward, I want you to hold every aspect of your life up to this why. If it is aligned, it gets to stay. If it is not, let it go.

2. Next, I give you permission to stop *"shoulding"* on yourself. Should is a word of abuse and inaction – you deserve better. Pay attention to when you hear the word "should" slipping out of your mouth and try restating the same thought in a different way.

3. Finally, surround yourself with support, both professionally and personally. Remember, you are one woman living one life. By nurturing and supporting all aspects of your being, you will achieve the life and business you desire. Now go show your business who's boss!

About the Author

As a Stanford graduate and Intel engineer turned homemaker and entrepreneur, Jocelyn knows the unique challenges of walking away from one's expected plan in life to create your own unique path.

Jocelyn has over a decade of experience building, running and wrangling a multi six figure WordPress Web Design Agency, working part-time while having two boys at home under the age of thirteen.

She jokes that she has a lot of balls in the air and a few rolling around on the floor.

Jocelyn's funny and authentic style makes her a powerful inspirational speaker and coach. Her "say it like it is" realness enables her to connect with audiences large and small. Attendees leave Jocelyn's talks inspired and ready to take action. If you want to connect with Jocelyn for coaching and business strategy or to bring her to your stage you can connect with her at: www.jocelynmozak.com/womenrising.

8

EMBODY YOUR SACRED ESSENCE AND OWN YOUR POWER

HOW I TRANSFORMED PAIN TO POWER

"Awakening to the true power living within accelerates your Divine purpose. You came to Earth to share your Essence and leave a legacy. Allow me to take you on a journey to heal your wounds and embody wholeness."
– Jessica Valor

From the time I was a young girl, with high hopes and big dreams, I was experiencing heavy trauma and abuse. I barely survived my childhood. I moved through adulthood with scraped knees and a bruised heart as my mode of operation for survival. In all of this space of growing, becoming and learning to trust, I found myself in each moment experiencing pain or fear, judgment or shame – losing the trust in who and what I truly was, little by little.

Yet despite this, I was tenacious. I would show up and put on a smile for life, but there was a disconnection from my truth, from my soul, and from my power. It was there, but I had learned to ignore the whispers from spirit and the calling deep within me, because it wasn't normal or safe to be me. I was denying a part of who I was.

Everything changed in a moment of deep loss. My best friend was my soulmate. We felt like we had lived many lifetimes together. His friendship was the insurance that everything would always be ok. He was that person that I could go to at any moment, at any time. He understood me to the core and he witnessed my wholeness. We were inseparable.

When I learned of his passing, my world crumbled. My heart shattered. I found myself on the floor, layered in tears, trembling, wondering what this was all for, and if I could even catch my breath to continue.

From this space of deep grief, pain and loss, I attempted to take my own life. And what happened next was my miracle.

In the sacred space in between life and death that had opened in an instant, I found myself filled with light in a ceremony in Heaven. I was surrounded by ascended masters who all shared with me that I had a divine purpose that was not yet fulfilled. My purpose was that I needed to show others that sacred space... to uncover and embody their own sacred essence and power... to know at their heart of hearts that they are supported, loved and guided... and that in all of their struggles, in all of the pain, that they are never, ever alone.

This was the message I needed to hear, and it is a message I know that the world needs to hear. We are in a place where the world needs healing. I came back from that near-death experience changed. I realized that all my life, I had denied my true self and my connection to something greater than me. Within that space of understanding, I found myself embodying the spiritual gifts I was given. I was able to cure the doubt that had walked beside me. I was able to learn how to let go, lead with courage and embody the essence of who and what I am.

As I look around the world today, I see so many people who are craving that deep spiritual connection, but are unsure of how to truly, trustingly embody and integrate it into their life's work and who they are.

I believe that what we all need right now is to lead with love and cure the doubt that we are not powerful, or that we have not received our divine gifts, or that we are not worthy of sharing them with the world.

I invite you to lean into LOVE, which is a sweet acronym for: Letting go, Omnipresence, Valor and Essence. If we can learn to let go of our own doubts, we will be free. We will create that sacred space of divinity where we are guided and can learn to forgive ourselves for the times where we haven't stepped fully into the higher version of who we are.

We are spiritual beings having a human experience. If you could tune in and understand that there is an omnipresent power within you, then nothing would stop you. Nothing would stand in your way. You would move forward with the calling that is living within you.

I believe that we are afraid of our own power. As women, we are afraid of being powerful, and we must step up into valor, into courage.

If we are to light the way for others, we need to awaken the courage within us to make it happen – by finding the essence of who we truly are, and what we are that no one else is. This essence is your magic.

My gift is to help you embody your essence so you no longer doubt, but you believe in the power that is you. You believe in the beauty that is you. You believe in the truth that is you, and you believe that there is no one else on this Earth that has your gifts.

What it comes down to is knowing the how behind our why. Even once we've learned to let go, embraced our omnipresence to lead with courage and embody our essence, we still have to understand that it takes alchemy actions to create a spiritual strategy, where we are integrating spiritual alignment into our everyday lives.

It is our divine birthright to step into this calling, integrate the presence of spirit into our lives and welcome it in with open arms. Yes, you need to open your heart, but also put up a big effing fence, because this is your life. This is your work. This is your time, and unless you understand your big why, your purpose, and you protect it with all the sacred energy and valor that you have, others will try to take you down and stop you from doing the work you are called to do. In all of what I have shared, I want you to feel the shift. I want you to feel the shift that can happen within you when you drop the doubts and lean into love.

You can take aligned alchemy actions in your life that lead you to a place where you no longer see spirit and your life's work as separate. You'll know without a shadow of a doubt that the only way you can do what you are here to do is by aligning and integrating the spiritual into your life. We are here for a purpose. We are creative leaders.

Rise Up Challenge

1. If you find yourself unsure of the steps to take to move into alignment, I invite you to make a list of what you are available for and not available for. This unmasks where your true commitments currently live.
2. Next, create a list of boundaries (this is your fence around your heart chakra) where you will commit to saying yes to you and no to anything not in alignment with your truth.
3. Step three, create a sacred contract with the Universe/God – list all of the things you desire to accomplish in service and what you desire to receive in return. Then, let it go to be delivered. This is where you will embody the divinity within you and trust.

Hidden fear and doubt will present themselves to you and be dissolved from your body through the process of these simple steps. Their appearance will require you to face the fears. This brings you to embody your power, and through this, you will become whole.

About the Author

Jessica Valor is an inspirational speaker, healer and mentor who delivers her programs to thousands of women and men every year on the topics of conscious leadership, intuitive intelligence and personal development.

Jessica is a clear and powerful conduit for High-level Spirits.

Jessica was an intuitive child and has always felt deeply connected to the Universal aspects of living. She awakened to the strengths of her clairvoyant, healing gifts in 2011 after her own near-death experience where she visited Heaven, met with a council of Ascended Masters and returned to life to help the world heal and move through ascension.

Jessica helps individuals, entrepreneurs and organizations connect to their inner wisdom and higher levels of awareness to craft the life or business they truly desire. She loves empowering her clients' intuitive abilities and dream visions, and brings forward their best ideas and desired outcomes.

Jessica believes we all have a deep knowing of who we are and what we want. With a little guidance and awakening, we are empowered to THRIVE.

When not inspiring thousands of leaders, Jessica is found as a domestic Goddess – cooking, creating rituals, practicing yoga and of course singing and dancing to her favorite songs with her fur baby, Monji, whom she adores. She loves helping her clients rise to their highest potential and builds the foundation of #teamlove to help those in need.

You can connect with Jessica and receive exclusive access to her Love Your Life library full of rituals, meditations (on the go) and alchemy eBooks to transform your life and manifest your desires at http://www.jessicavalor.com.

9

THE JOURNEY TOGETHER

HOW THE POWER OF CONNECTION CAN PROPEL US TO OUR NEXT LEVEL

"Having support and connections in our lives enables us to lean into each other and be empowered to move forward, dream bigger and accomplish more."
– Giselle Morell Marin

Unstable, unconventional, traumatic, but *full* of love. Those were my parents. Unstable, unconventional, traumatic, but *filled* with love. That was my childhood. Oxymoron, right? For part of my life, I could not understand how a house filled with so much instability and trauma could be a source of so much love and support. But as I grew, I learned that it came from the power of connection, support and love – and my belief in this power has become the driving force in my life.

For a large part of my childhood, I grew up in a house that was crippled and torn by addiction. This forced me, at a very young age, to step into a role that was much larger than my young self. At the age of eleven, I vividly remember being the financial guardian for my mom, ensuring that the money she earned was spent on our necessities before she could spend it on her addiction. I remember like it was yesterday. At the age of twelve, I was taking care of my siblings and ensuring that their basic needs were met when my parents couldn't fulfill that role.

When I was thirteen, my mom hit rock bottom. In an effort to hold on to us, the only thing she had left, she pulled herself out of that hole and into sobriety. Throughout my parents' addiction and illness, I had become their support. I was somewhat of a caretaker for them, as well as their north star.

As a mom to four kids of my own, I know now that these are big roles to step into for anyone, but especially for a child. Did I resent my parents? For a while I did. But I also know that addiction is an illness, that it can blind a person to do wrong even though everything in them wants to do the right thing. As a young child, I saw the pain in my parents' eyes, but I also felt the love they had for us pushing them and fueling them towards sobriety.

The year my mom found sobriety was a pivotal turning point in my life and in our relationship. Yes, it was a big move forward into a semblance of "normalcy" for my siblings and I. But it was also a drastic change to what had previously been our "normal." I found myself at thirteen years old with a mom who was ready to fully step into her role, but because of all the years that were lost, we didn't know exactly how the mom/daughter relationship was supposed to work.

So, we created our own unconventional mother/daughter relationship. We became more than mother/daughter, and more than friends. A mother is supposed to be the caregiver to a child, but since I had taken the role of caring for her for a time, in an odd way, that role reversal created an even stronger bond – one that very few could ever understand. My mom became an incredible force in my life.

When I was twenty-five, with a flourishing career and a loving family, my world suddenly came to a screeching halt. My mom passed away from stomach cancer at the young age of forty-five. She had become such an incredible source of support for me that the loss was unbearable. My dad felt so lost without her that within a short twelve months he passed away from a broken heart. My teenage siblings were left without parents and in my care. A responsibility I was all too familiar with, but that I took on willingly, full heartedly and gratefully.

Only through grace, love and an incredible amount of support was I able to overcome this truly debilitating and dark time in my life. While overcoming all these obstacles and challenges, I quickly came to understand two very important lessons. The first is that we are not meant to do it alone. Can we do it alone? Yes, absolutely. But having support and connections in our lives enables us to lean into each other and be empowered to move forward, dream bigger and accomplish more. In my most dark moments, having support was instrumental in coming back into the light.

Secondly, I began to fully understand that each and every one of us have been given innate gifts and strengths that are developed and nurtured through our environment, experiences and circumstances. Life then gives us the choice – to be deflated by our experience and circumstances – or to use them to fully step into our gifts, our calling, and into who we truly are. I chose the latter.

As my career continued to flourish, I began to see the commonality of these two lessons. I integrated them into both areas of my life – professionally, and in my personal life in my roles as a mom, wife, sister and friend. I could now clearly see the importance and power of connection, support and community – these are needed to carry and push you forward successfully.

Professionally, I spent the next fifteen years in a large Fortune 500 company, where part of my responsibility was creating and supporting events of many different sizes and areas of focus. Through my tenure in creating events, I witnessed first hand how meaningful and impactful both personal and professional events can be. These events had one very special thing in common – their success was built on creating a sense of community, a bond of support and in some cases, a sense of family. This realization aligned perfectly with my own greatest values – family and connection. I value being a mom, wife, daughter, sister and friend above all else. I believe in the power of community and gathering. The power of creating beautiful, impactful experiences where memories are forged.

So, in 2015 I launched Dreamality Events. It is an event planning company that focuses on supporting and enabling people to create events and experiences with the client journey in mind.

Disney World is known to be the happiest place on earth. They create an experience in every single moment by focusing on every part of the customer's journey – from the moment you walk through those big, shining gates, to standing in line for a ride, to each ride and other type of entertainment, even to the moment you leave. Every detail of the journey from start to finish creates a special experience.

That is my goal – that each event created consistently delivers the client's desired experience on each step of the journey. Zeroing in on what they should feel before, during and after the event. Truly creating an experience they will never forget.

This is my passion. Helping people create spaces and events that make an impact beyond just the time that they are together. Forging real, lasting relationships, connections and collaborations that continue to impact their own life, their companies, families, relationships and beyond.

I see what is possible, if only we choose to not go at it alone, to be supported in our work, to know that we are supported and that someone is there for us. This gives us such peace of mind.

We can then focus on the big vision, the deeper work. We can create one cohesive experience that brings us together and helps us all to make a bigger impact in the world.

Whether you are thinking about hosting your own event, or whether you are struggling in your personal life, I want you to remember that you do not have to do it alone. Know that each of your experiences in life have led you right here, to this moment in time.

Every struggle, every hardship comes with a blessing or lesson that can help you grow and become who you are truly meant to be. As you step out into the world, always remember – in everything you do, you too can turn an ordinary experience into a moment where dreams come true!

Rise Up Challenge

1. Create a list of areas or projects, both in your personal and professional life, where you could use additional support.
2. How can your business or your personal life benefit from freeing up some of your time?
3. Write down 1-3 people for each project whose support/service you feel could benefit you. Connect with these people.

About the Author

With over a decade of event management experience, a knack for fixing problems with smart, inventive ideas and an "anything is possible" attitude, Giselle became the founder of Dreamality Events – an event planning and management company. Giselle believes in working together with her clients to transform their events from idea to experience, producing heart centered events that inspire, connect and have a lasting impact on both the audience and the host.

Giselle has a broad range of event planning experience. She has produced events for a wide variety of clients – large Fortune 500 companies, startups, nonprofits and individuals. In her tenure she's managed galas, conferences, dinner events and retreats ranging from twenty-five to several hundred attendees. Giselle currently holds her CMP certification and is a published author.

As a wife and busy mom of four, Giselle also knows what it's like to lose yourself in the everyday trenches of motherhood. Through the challenges of raising a family while managing a career, Giselle quickly learned the importance of self-care, self-love and support for moms. With a passion for helping women in the same trenches, Giselle founded The Mom-Volution Project – a network of women motivating and supporting each other to "do motherhood" in a new and empowering way. To connect with Giselle, visit www.gisellemmarin.com.

10

THE DEFINING MOMENT

WHAT IS KEEPING YOU FROM THE LIFE YOU WANT
TO CREATE?

*"You know, it feels good. To be proud of my success and what I
have achieved. To be proud of breaking the pattern of my family.
To be proud of who I have become."*
– Julie Fairhurst

How do you succeed with no support? How do you deal with a
past of chaos, negativity and craziness? Have you wondered why
some people are successful, while others, even from the same
family, can end up homeless drug addicts, living a life of crime?

I remember very little happiness as a child. The emotional abuse
in my family was rampant. Messages like, "If it wasn't for you
kids, I wouldn't drink." "You kids just suck the money out of me,
it's no wonder I'm always broke." "None of you will ever
amount to anything."

From the time I was a little girl, in every circumstance, every challenge I found myself in, I knew something was wrong. I remember telling myself when I was as young as five years old, *I'm not going to be like them when I'm older.* At that young age, I had already chosen to be different.

My teen years were rocky, with drug abuse, a teen pregnancy, dropping out of school and living on welfare. Although I knew I could do better and I wanted to do better, I lacked the skills and support needed to change.

Then one day, I read a story that resonated with me. It changed my mindset forever. I call this my "wake up moment." It caused me to turn towards a different path than the one I was on.

The story was about two brothers.

One brother was living a life of success – great career, loving family, living with amazing values. The other brother was living a life of crime – in jail for committing murder – following in the footsteps of his father who also incarcerated for murder.

These brothers had come from the same gene pool, same family, same circumstances, yet were living entirely different lives.

During the interviews, they were asked identical questions. One question jumped out at me and stirred my curiosity. The question that they were asked was answered exactly the same way by both brothers.

"Why did you turn out the way you did?" the interviewer asked.

Both responded, "With a family like mine, how else would you expect me to turn out?"

This was my wake up moment. It was the moment I knew that I

had the power in me to break patterns, to choose the path I was going to walk. It was then that I decided to take responsibility for where I was and where I was going. I knew I could choose positive experiences no matter what negative crap had been a part of my life. There would be no more excuses for why I could not live the life of my dreams.

I realised I needed to change my mindset! It wasn't easy. Working on myself required a lot of perseverance. I've read that for every negative comment said to you, you need five positive comments to erase it – and I had experienced so many negatives.

I knew I had to start telling a different story to myself than the one I was living.

So, I went to work, on me. Every single day I was plugging in those cassette tapes, putting in those CDs, reading those books – ones that would infuse my brain and my subconscious with positivity, with affirmations... changing the stories I was telling myself and the world... breaking patterns, leading me to fulfill my vision of exactly who I wanted to be and the life I wanted to create.

You see, I've had massive success in my life. If you were to look back at my history, at the way I was raised, at the places I've lived and circumstances I've been in, some would say that it is quite a miracle. However, I would say the truth is that this miracle resides in all of us. It's that moment when we decide to choose success over struggles.

I was struggling in life – I wanted to do better. I wanted to have independence and freedom. I decided I wanted to have it all, that I was worthy of having it all, and I deserved it.

So, I quit my job and decided to be an entrepreneur. I researched and decided sales would give me the flexibility I was looking for and the income I was wanting. I decided going into real estate was my best option.

There were huge mind shifts I had to go through to find my path to success. I didn't even know anyone who owned real estate, so it was a total leap of faith.

To go from standing in line at food banks and living off government handouts to becoming the top real estate agent in my office, selling over a quarter of a billion dollars in real estate… to be included in the elite group of the top 1% of agents in my area, as well as my company, across the country… marketing multimillion-dollar housing developments for some of the most successful developers in the country – I'd achieved my goals and the life I envisioned for myself.

What are the dreams that you are not living? What's holding you back? What story are you telling about yourself? Are you stuck in the same old story? Living in the same old pattern? Are you following your dreams, or walking in the footsteps of your past generation?

I know deep down that no matter what, every single one of you can choose to create the life that was meant for you.

When you tell a different story – shift your beliefs, stop blaming, stop making excuses, start to take responsibly, live in the present (not the past), shift your thinking from lack to abundance, have appreciation and gratitude – now you have the keys for success.

In my life, I stay conscious of where I am going, constantly looking forward. Looking at my past is not going to help me achieve my dreams and goals. It will only keep me stuck.

My life today is black and white different from the life I was headed towards. I was on the same path as my family before me, and would have ended up there too, had I not started taking responsibility for my life – both my past and my future.

You know, it feels good. To be proud of my success and what I have achieved. To be proud of breaking the pattern of my family. To be proud of who I have become.

Often, we look for tools for success – how to create more income and live a life of fulfillment. But we skip over the one thing I believe is truly the most important – our mindset. I believe mindset comes first, tools are secondary. Without the right mindset, your tools can't help you.

My favourite word is Believe! Believe in yourself. Believe you can do anything you set your mind to. Believe you are worthy of success and all that comes with it.

I help others shift what they believe is possible and create wealth on their terms. This is why I do what I do – I know there is great power within each of us to choose our reality, to decide our future, to create financial freedom and change our story, no matter what our circumstance.

Rise Up Challenge

1. What do you want your life to look like? Write it out, read it to yourself often. Imagine what it would feel like to be there already. There is power in your feelings.
2. If you have fallen down, that's okay, but get back up,

dust yourself off and carry on. We all fall down from time to time, just don't stay down.

3. Do something for yourself that you have been putting off. Start taking care of you and treating yourself with love and kindness. Know you are worthy of having it all.

About the Author

Single mother of three, Julie survived on food banks and government handouts. Worried about the financial strain on her family, she knew she needed to do something – either quit or get on with it – but Julie was no quitter. Stopping the excuses, she discovered strategies to succeed.

Julie owns Rock Star Strategies, helping others find success in business and their personal lives. Using over twenty-seven years of award winning sales success, she's taken her secret strategies and developed a step by step program, so you too can have the strategies to achieve the success you desire.

Julie is included in an elite group of the top 1% of agents across the country, consistently top in her field, selling over a quarter of a billion dollars in real estate, as well as marketing and selling multimillion-dollar developments.

From business people to nursing students, from police officers to woman in recovery, Julie has inspired change through her speaking and training programs.

Are you ready to make your shift? Are you ready to grow an amazing business? Together with Julie, you can make it happen. For your free resource, go to www.rockstarstrategies.com.

11

SO LONG, AND THANKS FOR ALL THE FISH

HOW FINDING THE COURAGE TO WALK AWAY CHANGED MY LIFE AND HELPED ME TO REALIZE THAT IT IS NEVER TOO LATE...

"Learn to let go and create space – space to allow new opportunities to enter your life, whether they will be for business or for pleasure. It has taken me a long time to really understand this, and I am grateful EVERY day that I have. Travel light my friends."
– Annie Doherty

Have you ever held a baby bird and felt its heart rapidly beating within your hands? That's how mine felt, that sunny morning in the hotel room when I heard the words that seemed to etch themselves into my heart with a red-hot poker:

"Yeah, me too, I HATE being here, and I cannot wait to get back to you. I miss you."

I couldn't breathe. As soon as the hotel door closed after my

75

three shiny, happy girls skipped to meet their friends for breakfast, my husband had terminated the work call that he was on and redialed. I was trying to be oh so quiet, so that he wouldn't know that I hadn't gone down to breakfast with the girls. Or that I had just overheard a conversation I was not meant to hear.

I held my breath. Months of ignoring my sixth sense, gut, intuition, third eye and everything else in the universe that was shouting at me "Open your eyes and see!" was condensed down to me quietly hiding on the sofa behind the wall, holding my breath, waiting for my heart to break.

I'd been not wanting to believe it, but there it was, three simple little words, innocuous on their own – not even I LOVE YOU, but I MISS YOU. They were enough to shake my world to the core.

There was the expected messiness – he seemed shocked that I'd found out, I was a teetering volcano of emotion. I couldn't break down too much as I didn't want to upset my girls and spoil their summer holiday. Luckily I had a friend who was able to distract the girls so that I could walk the beach and try to make sense of my life. I thought:

When will I learn to listen with more than my ears?

Listen to your gut. If your intuition is waving a red flag, NOTICE IT!!

My daughters were young and I didn't want to bring them up without a dad. He seemed contrite, and I loved him. We tried again. To help us move on, we decided to move – not only houses, but countries. Friends thought we were crazy. Many didn't know the reason why we were doing this.

Hindsight is a fantastic thing. I now realize we were both just running from our problem, instead of turning around and facing it. You know the sneaky thing about problems? They follow you! So, after many years of travelling and living in different houses (including an exceptional dream home we built and then reluctantly sold due to the 2008 economic crash) I realized that to create change in my life, I had to take action.

Don't have regrets because you didn't take action.

As the girls grew and stretched their wings, some of them chose to return to the UK. I knew travel was again in my future, but the type of travel was way more significant than even I could guess. Early on in this year, as I was dragging my suitcase into the hall of my UK apartment, I tiredly wondered how many years of travelling I would have left before it all became too much. Would I get too tired to haul my suitcases and backpacks?

I was aware of a sense of the clocks running faster in the background of my mind. I was tired, but still smiled when I walked into my apartment. It was my safe place, my sanctuary. It was a little surreal coming back to the same familiar home after living in so many different houses. While each one had taught me amazing lessons, this little place had become as comfortable as a second skin.

The phone rang. "Mrs. Doherty, we are just calling to remind you that your repayment date is in six months. We wondered if you could tell us what financial instrument you will be using to clear the mortgage?"

Wait, what??

My husband had "given" me this perfect apartment, but omitted telling me it came with an interest-free mortgage that had to be clear, in full, the day before my sixty-third birthday.

So, here I was – the home stager who now has to stage my own beautiful apartment that hugs me when I walk through the door. I had to put my emotions aside and present my home in its best light so that it would be loved by another.

Then, I'll go travelling! I thought. Travel has become an undercurrent flowing through my life. I jokingly said to a friend recently that I could become "The Nomadic GrAnnie."

While that thought has now settled and isn't going anywhere soon, my next step was to take a leap of faith – I started a new business. I decided it was **never too late** to start again in my working life.

When we have listened with more than our ears to one and all and evaluated our decisions, we then plan the actions we know in our gut that we need to take. Sometimes though, we only see the immediate aftermath. Look further forward than that and see the bright potential that you and your life can embrace. I believe it is indeed **never too late**.

Next I decided, why not also apply this to where I live? I could give up most of my possessions (this lightens the chains of stuff that we drag around with us) and say "So long, and thanks for all the fish" – just like the dolphins did as they left earth in book four of *The Hitchhiker's Guide to The Galaxy*.

So, for now, I am following my gut and taking action. Feeling that, like the dolphins, I could walk away without a backwards glance, knowing that it is really **never too late**.

Rise Up Challenge

Journaling/writing exercises:

1. Listen with more than your ears. Trust your gut.

Over our lifetime, in both our business and personal lives, we will be "told" a lot of information. People may try to influence or coax you with their words to their way of thinking. Some, especially family members, can be very persuasive. There is a saying I'm sure you will have heard: "Listen to what they say, but watch what they do."

Along with watching, check in on yourself. Go to your hot spot. We all have one... that place in your body that reacts to truth, heartache, lies. We often just stopped listening. Get into the practice of checking in with yourself regularly.

Think of a time that you didn't listen with more than your ears – a situation where in hindsight, you knew that if you had, it would have saved you a lot of harsh lessons. Write this down.

How can you start NOW, today, to increase trust in your gut feelings little by little, and listen with more than your ears? Write this down.

2. Remember that if you want change to occur in your life, you have to take action.

STOP.

Take some quiet time and look at where you feel your life or business could be better.

Step back. Analyze.

Create a plan, write it down and then take action.

If you get stuck, ask yourself this: "If you could live your life again, what would you change?"

If something resonates with you, explore and write it down. Plan, then take action to create the change you desire.

3. It's never too late to...

Grow, live, love, have adventures, do whatever you can dream of. Think of this almost as a bucket list: write down your thoughts, no matter what, as they pop into your head. Then remember...

It is never too late.

Don't have regrets because you didn't take a chance.

About the Author

International award-winning Stager and Designer Annie Doherty cannot remember a time when she wasn't interested in colour, décor and design. Annie loves her creative life, and she enjoys nothing more than helping others solve property problems and design dilemmas, as well as assisting entrepreneurs to build their new businesses.

As a trainer for the House Doctor™ Network since 2006, Annie has written and presented numerous design and staging workshops and master classes as well as industry breakout talks both in the UK and the USA.

Having articles published in many design magazines such as

House Beautiful and Essex Life, as well as speaking in guest spots on BBC Radio, have helped establish Annie as the go-to expert. This led to Annie being featured as one of the Design and Staging experts in various home shows, such as Grand Designs and The Ideal Home Show.

Annie's message goes beyond just her expertise in design and staging. After living in twenty-three houses, in addition to life throwing her a few curve balls along the way, she vulnerably shares her insights and lessons that can be used by all in both business and life.

For more information or to request her e-book, please email annie@housedoctor.co.uk.

12

WAKE UP TO YOUR LIFE

FOLLOW YOUR OWN COMPASS AND LEARN TO TRUST YOURSELF AGAIN!

"Self-care is not indulgent... it's essential. When your needs are met and self-care is a non-negotiable priority, you can come to the world as the best version of yourself. Trusting yourself begins by taking care of yourself."
— Jo-Ann Brine

Have you ever found yourself wondering why you keep doing the things you do? Do you struggle to find balance? Do you find yourself continuing to search for that one person who will pat you on the head and tell you you're doing okay?

I know I did, and guess where I found her? In my mirror.

Seeking acceptance and external validation is polluting to our souls. It took me forty years to understand this.

I remember the first time I walked into Weight Watchers. I was the youngest person there. This was my first diet. I was twelve years old.

Looking back at my twelve-year-old self, I realize that this need to gain acceptance, recognition and validation had already become my default feedback loop. I was addicted to the stickers and the praise. I did lose eighteen pounds that summer, but I was motivated solely by outside validation and praise – things I had no idea how to give myself.

That was the first time that I dieted, but it was definitely not the last. In this cycle, the self-judgment and self-loathing began. I became dependant on pleasing the person weighing me. They would tell me whether I was good enough (or not!). This was the beginning of my professional on-again/off-again dieting "career." Too bad we don't get paid for these experiences, huh?

This need for validation trickled into the way I built my career. I was driven to "win the gold star sticker." I wanted to be all things to all people. Super-mom. Super-wife. Super-friend. Super-leader. Super-daughter. Super-_____ (fill in the blank).

I went on to build a "super" career, but it was generated from everything outside of myself. I continued to be dependent on other people evaluating whether or not I was good enough. I kept looking for everyone else to tell me where I should go next. I had zero self-trust. I didn't believe that I knew what was best for me. I had no idea how to tune in and listen to the beautiful voice that lived *deep* within me.

I remember being on the road a lot. My son was four, so whenever I could, I would try to make it home so he could wake up to his momma – or, I would leave after tucking him in! I vividly remember my face-down moment. It was at a B&B in Newfoundland. I had gotten up to go to the washroom to get a cold cloth because I wasn't feeling great… and that is the last thing I remember. I woke up, reached for my pillow, and realized I was literally, face down on the floor. I remember trying to get back up into bed – but once again, I fell face down. I had an awareness of what was happening, but I was helpless to do anything about it.

It was so weird. Almost like an out of body experience. A guest from the room below knocked on the door to see if I was okay. She had heard the big thumps. I answered the door, assuming I was okay, and the lady gasped and said, "We better get you to the hospital." I had unknowingly split my chin open and was bleeding on the floor. The confusion and fear I felt were overwhelming. What if I hadn't woken up?

I was scared. I was alone. I could only think, *What would happen to my little boy without his mother?*

After several stitches and a myriad of tests, the results showed nothing. "You are simply exhausted."

Wow.

This is what my life had become. An exhausted wife, mother and career woman who was constantly striving for perfection. I never allowed myself time to rest. I refused to loosen the reins on my need to "control" situations (like always putting my son to bed). Because I was constantly looking for approval and validation from others, I was always finding myself in places I didn't want to be. Like face down in a hotel room.

Hello, wake-up call! I remember thinking to myself, "Holy shit

Jo-Ann, you better start taking care of yourself. You matter to a lot of people, why don't you matter to yourself? You've got to figure out some kind of balance in your life."

Balance? Who has time for that?

Gulp. I had a long way to go!

Once I started tuning in to what *I* wanted, and how *I* wanted to feel, the journey became less daunting.

My life took a complete 180. I started taking care of myself. I started paying attention to that inner voice. I recreated my life. I became aware that wholeness was *possible*! How exciting! This triggered a desire to help other women who struggle on a similar hamster wheel. As a result, I became a yoga teacher and Transformational Health Coach. I created a life for myself that represented balance – where the connection between the mind, body, emotions and soul + spirit became integrated.

There is richness in this approach. Once I integrated these four areas into my daily self-care practices, I wholeheartedly believed I was as successful on the outside as I now knew myself to be on the inside. My inner voice was the leader of my life, not the other way around. I had kicked the need for approval and validation to the curb (mostly)! I felt connected to myself. I felt whole. My soul was no longer polluted.

Here is my invitation to you – this is the time to wake up to what's really going on in your life. You only have this one life.

Dig in. Ditch your limiting beliefs. As a twelve-year-old, I used "diets" and weight loss as my worthiness guide. I continued into adulthood to look outside of myself for love, respect and trust. What a load of *bull*!

Like me, you need to look closely at your life to see where your stories and beliefs come from. You need to heal your wounds so that you can truly start to move forward. You need to understand that your emotions are generated from your thoughts, and that your self-talk dictates how you feel and act. The results you're getting are a reflection of your actions. You see, I was numbing and distracting myself with food. I was hiding behind food to avoid being responsible for my life. Your distractions may be different. You may be working long hours, binge watching Netflix, endlessly tapping into social media or just coasting along, unaware that loving life is possible. Only you can *wake up to your life*. You need to do the work to recognize the patterns, stories and beliefs that are getting in the way.

I challenge you to stop running, hiding and numbing. Pause and sit with your uncomfortable emotions. Feel them. Get comfortable feeling uncomfortable. Then, each time you feel an emotion that isn't what you want, get clear on what the thought was that came right before it. This will get you started on the path to self-discovery. It will help you identify the power your thoughts have on your emotions. We need to feel. Not numb. When you numb the uncomfortable feelings, you also numb the joyful ones.

You won't find an exact action plan here. Instead, I want you to guide yourself. Tune into your own compass. Find your version of wholeness. Find your truth in self-trust. Self-trust strips away judgment, perfectionism and pleasing others.

When you lean into trusting yourself and following your own compass, you will be creating a life you love.

Rise Up Challenge

Shift from doing what you think you should be doing to what your heart loves…

1. What are you doing for others or for the sticker, the praise, the outward validation?
2. What are you doing that you feel you *should* be doing?
3. What would you love to be doing instead?
4. What practices can you start doing that will help you *wake up to your life*?

About the Author

Jo-Ann is a lifestyle and business coach, author, speaker and the co-founder of Leaderista. She is on a mission to help women wake up to their lives and become the best version of themselves.

After becoming a certified transformational nutrition coach and certified yoga teacher, Jo-Ann led many workshops and retreats. She has been a featured expert on The Transformational Health Summit and the Simplify Your Summer tele-summit.

Jo-Ann has helped over a hundred women connect to their bodies through mindfulness, movement and gentle nutrition – freeing them from the never-ending diet trap and teaching them to make themselves a priority. She integrates mind, body and spirit practices. She is here to help women break free from the constant search for external validation. She empowers women to move

from self-doubt to self-trust by showing them how to go inward, get quiet and listen for the answers that lie within... to learn to follow their own compass.

Jo-Ann is also a mom and a wife. She loves to spend time with family and has regular coffee dates with friends. She believes in balance – she loves coffee and wine, and also makes a killer green smoothie! And yes, Jo-Ann *can* do ALL this because she makes sure she is on her own to-do list. Learn more about Jo-Ann's work at www.leaderista.com.

13

PERMISSION TO PROSPER

HOW GOING ALL IN SAVED MY LIFE

"How can I possibly look my daughter in the eye and tell her to go after her dreams when I am not doing the same?"
– Alison Beierlein

You know how as a teenager, you get so preoccupied trying to figure out who you really are, that the rest of the world seems to speed past and you hardly take notice? I felt that way. I was saving up money to move abroad and travel. As soon as I finished school, I moved to Europe.

Less than a year later, I got a call from my mom. I had been working at a botanical garden – it was hot and I was exhausted. All I wanted to do was have a cold shower and a glass of rose. When I took the call, something was off. She asked me to sit down. My heart was pounding hard in my chest as I waited for her news.

She told me my dad had died. He ended his own life. It felt

unreal, like I was being transported back to earth at warp speed. He was my dad, and now he was gone. In fact, we hadn't spoken in months. I know now that he had stopped talking to me because he didn't know how to handle the stress that he was feeling. The stress I caused because he was worried about money. That made it so much worse.

Time passed and I worked through my grief. I felt nervous about ever really putting myself out there again. I went with "ok" instead so I would never have to feel the guilt I felt the last time I put myself first and went after my dreams.

I grew up and got married. My husband and I were getting by. I wouldn't call it poverty by any means, but we definitely weren't rolling in the dough. Middle class, they call it. I was playing small and going through the motions. Eat, work, sleep, do housework. Wash, rinse, repeat.

I should be grateful, though, right? Isn't that what they say? Practice gratitude.

We started our family and I was grateful, truly, but I became more and more entrenched in my role as the giver. I was the provider. I was the glue that held our family together. My own passions, desires and personality were dimmed so low you could hardly see them.

Who had I become? Where was that smart young girl who could pursue any goal that she could dream of? I hadn't seen her in a very, very long time. Why wasn't I living with the same level of success as others around me were, when I knew I had it in me? There was this inner battle between being grateful for what I had – two healthy children, a loving and loyal husband, a salary – and wanting more.

I felt unfulfilled and torn inside. I felt guilty for even thinking that what I had wasn't enough. *My kids are healthy – isn't that all that matters?*

I realized, if I am not pursuing my passions and going after all of my desires with my best effort, I am not living with integrity. How could I possibly look my daughter in the eye and tell her to go after her dreams when *I* was not doing the same? She needs a strong, fierce role model who rises up and shows her everything that is possible when she goes all in.

In early 2016 I discovered the world of online business. It was as though someone finally flicked the light on in my life and showed me how to turn things around. I began giving myself permission to do work that I loved AND make a great living AND spend more time with my kids.

Over the next two years, I sacrificed. I worked late. I worked early. I worked my butt off. It was freeing and terrifying and exciting all in one. It was a season of determination and hustle.

It certainly wasn't a smooth ride. I questioned and doubted myself. I felt unsure and insecure. I worried about what people would say. I worried I might fail. And so, the roller coaster of an emotional ride continued until the time finally came when I went all in – I left my 9-5 behind and haven't looked back.

Now, I no longer commute endless hours every week to work on building and maintaining someone else's empire. I am building my own. I am showing my daughter what is possible when you say "yes" to living in pursuit of your own authentic desires. But

I'd be lying if I told you it was easy. What I can tell you is what I learned.

It all started with the approval. The permission. The green light that allowed me to shed the guilt I was feeling for wanting more, and to stop telling myself that it was too late in my life to turn things around.

This took a lot of inner work. I began journaling. I became a self-development junkie. I went from thinking mindset work was a bunch of woo-woo garbage to seeing how it was the key to my success. You have to change your brain if you want to change your life.

What followed next was releasing the "how." My analytical mind was starving for a concrete plan. My need for control wanted to know exactly how I would build this business. It wasn't until I released this idea of having it all perfect that the magic truly started to happen. In the space of allowing myself the time and freedom to try things out and pivot my direction, I finally achieved clarity in how I would make this business become a reality.

And when I was ready, I got support. I knew deep down that if I was going to take this on and do the thing that would require me to hang my head out, way past the boundaries of my comfort zone, I was going to need the accountability, cheerleading and mentorship from someone who could help me get out of my own way.

Looking back, I see that I needed to hit bottom before that reality would be powerful enough to motivate me to the point of taking all of these uncomfortable action steps.

Fast forward to today – I now help other women to claim their own desires and make them happen. Too often I see successful women holding themselves back from even daring to dream the big dreams. I see the woman who has it in her to change the world, but is stalling, because her business feels overwhelming and she doesn't see a clear path to get her to where she needs to be. I give them permission to ditch the guilt and realize that the more they prosper, the more good they can do in the world. Helping women rise and thrive, while going after my own dreams, is the example I want to give to my daughter and to all the women I am honoured to support on their journey.

Rise Up Challenge

1. How much more of an impact could you make to better this world, if money wasn't an issue? Write out ten ways you can make a positive impact. It's OK to want to play big. You have permission to prosper.
2. When you are unsure how to move forward in your business, find your action steps by looking at the end goal. Then work backwards from there, one step at a time.
3. Now build those bridges. Compare where your business is now with where you want it to be. What supporting projects could you complete to close those gaps? Start there and take it one step at a time.

About the Author

Alison Beierlein uses her more than a decade of international experience in business development, sales and operations management as a Certified Business Coach and Consultant. She helps six-figure entrepreneurs grow into confident seven-figure business owners. She brings a well-rounded approach to her work that gets results that are aligned with her clients' professional and personal goals.

Whether they're struggling with how to bring on their first (or more) team member(s), how to increase their revenue or how to create systems that will allow them more freedom to focus on the parts of the business they love, Alison helps business owners create a scalable model that creates a bigger impact (and more cash in the bank).

When Alison isn't helping her clients multiply their income, she's playing Go Fish with her daughter, teaching her son how to ride his bike and enjoying the backcountry views around a campfire.

Ready to start scaling your business? Get free resources at www.alisonbeierlein.com.

14

A COLLISION COURSE TO ONENESS

HOW MY SEARCH FOR MEANING LED ME TO REDEFINE BUSINESS AND FIND MY PURPOSE

"It is your birthright to flourish. Embrace your business and your spiritual path as one. Leverage your business, not only for wealth, but for your own ascension."
– Donna Brown

This is the story of my search for meaning – how two different paths, business and spiritual, led to one destination. This is some of what I have gleaned in my attempt to answer those universal questions: who am I, why am I here, what am I meant to do?

Growing up, I had a difficult childhood. As I became a wife and mother, there were many struggles within that dynamic as well. On many days, I seemed to be at a breaking point. There were times I didn't think I would make it.

I knew that if something didn't change, I was in serious trouble. That deep connection to myself was lost and I had no idea why I was here. Caught up in the stories, in the lies and beliefs of others, I had forgotten how truly strong I am – that I have gifts to be shared, and that I have the right to be happy and to flourish.

Throughout all of these challenges, I learned to compartmentalise my life. I put my business in one container, my spiritual life in another and my relationships in yet another. I kept them as separate as possible in an effort to find an oasis of something akin to happiness or fulfillment, however fleeting. Thriving in my professional world, miserable in my private life, things didn't make sense.

I was constantly searching for that One Thing that would define me and shape my professional life – something I could settle into and call my own. My search led me through a wide variety of careers: classical musician, designer of fashion, gardens and home furnishings, TV personality, cookbook author and even gelato expert.

My imposter syndrome was through the roof as I tried to make sense of these beautiful opportunities that seemed to have no connection with one another.

Instinctively, I felt the labels – designer, consultant, TV host, author – could not describe me as a person. They could not capture what I felt was my purpose. Yet we search for and hang onto these labels. We deliberately cut up our lives into bite-sized chunks. I remember feeling exhausted and confused, trying to make sense of things as I moved from one job to another.

On the one hand I was miserable in my personal life – on the other, I couldn't make sense of what I was supposed to do for a living.

These two quests were on a collision course that ended with me in a heap of tears, asking what my purpose was. Through a very gifted friend of mine, this is the channeled message I received:

"Life isn't a highway. You don't get on at the on-ramp and drive straight until you get off when you die. What if you were to see life as a walk in the garden, as an invitation to explore?"

This message was such a relief and marked the beginning of my freedom. Once I let go of the search for a label to define me, I was able to see that what we call purpose is more a way of *being* rather than *doing*. Things fell into place. I am a designer – of businesses, products and places. A creative visionary, who through her intuition facilitates the birthing of what other people are meant to create. I find their blocks, their missed opportunities, and where they have gotten lost. I bring them to clarity, joy and revenue.

As the business and spiritual paths merged, everything changed. I dove deeper and deeper into my journey to awakening, and my view of business and its true purpose shifted completely. A sacred shift. I began to understand that what we call business is really a channel, a medium of expression for our highest selves.

As my holistic vision of life and business deepened, I applied the spiritual principles of generosity, compassion and intention in my business. I began making offerings of my work. I saw and felt incredible results – in my happiness, in my sense of fulfillment, in my revenue and opportunities – so I began to share these practices with my clients.

Every moment, every action is sacred – or more precisely, as sacred as we choose to make it. I realized what a powerful tool business can be in our spiritual quest, not just the other way round.

I was able to help my clients leverage their spiritual practice to super scale their business. The results are incredible. Super scaling your business isn't about serving more people. It can be, but what it really means is amplifying who you are and how you show up in the world by tapping into your root essence – and then bringing this forth in all its magnificence. Helping others realize this is my purpose, my mission and my hope for each and every one of you.

Imagine a majestic oak tree. Its root system matches the canopy. If it didn't, the tree would topple over. The deeper we go inwards, the higher we will be able to soar. We need to find out "how" we serve others even more deeply than "why." Leading from this place of truth and connection to who we are at our essence becomes the wellspring of joy, self-sovereignty and abundance.

How would things change if you were to see your business as a form of self-expression?

Your business is an amplification of you in your purest, most enlightened form. I invite you to let go of everything you have ever thought about business and making money. Embrace the idea of your business as an essential part of your path to awakening.

What does this really mean from a practical point of view? One of the most powerful practices I share with my clients is how to make an offering of your work and imbue it with intention, even if you are paid top dollar for this service. This practice stems directly from the Tibetan Buddhist tradition. Before doing anything – an email, an offer, a speech or even a book chapter – you dedicate it not only to the direct recipients, but to the benefit of all beings.

This shift in intention moves you from your head and ego into your heart. Instead of worrying if people will like you, or buy your product, you move into a space of generosity, compassion and service. This immediately reduces stress and provides a level of fulfilment, whatever the outcome.

Understanding the nature of purpose and embracing your business as a spiritual practice may sound abstract. You may think this is difficult to put into action. Nothing could be further from the truth. Everything we dream and desire needs action to become a reality.

I have had clients who understand the true nature of their purpose and business increase the ROI (return on investment) on their Facebook ads 600% in one week, triple their income in six months, and make a shift from having a multiple six-figure blog to running an eight-figure lifestyle brand and e-commerce website.

Spirituality is an eminently practical experience that is meant to improve your life in all its aspects and manifestation. It helps us become our own source of love, compassion and wisdom, giving us the freedom to choose how we will act and react – and that is the true source of our abundance and liberation. From this wellspring will flow the abundance, impact and fulfillment you seek in your business and your life.

Dive deep into who you are, your connection to yourself and the Universe.

Leverage your business for your path to awakening and leverage your awakening to grow your business.

Rise Up Challenge

1. Write a list of all the things you love to do, even if they seem to have nothing in common. Is there a way of *being* beneath the labels that feels like you? Your description of who you are will show up as broader, archetypal terms that are imbued with purpose – such as mentor, nurturer, visionary or creative. Are you bringing this way of being into your life and your work? If not, how can you change that?

2. Once a day, choose one thing related to your business and offer it for the benefit of all beings. An example could be, "May this offer be for the highest benefit of the receiver, but also for all beings that come into contact with this offer, directly or indirectly. May they receive wisdom, inspiration and support as if they have worked with the most perfect mentor." Notice and journal how this action shifts your perspective and what results it brings.

About the Author

Donna Brown is a business designer, growth strategist, business visionary and speaker. After decades of experience in the design, media and business worlds, Donna learned to combine her spiritual search and studies. She has become equally at home showing you how to apply powerful spiritual practices in your life and business as she is at creating a unique business model

that will allow you to super scale.

Donna's deepest desire and heart's work is for each of us to be happy and live a meaningful life. She sees business as a form of self-expression and a powerful tool on the path to enlightenment. There is nothing she loves more than brainstorming and sharing infinite possibilities over a beautiful home-made meal and a glass of wine.

To receive a free copy of "How to Achieve Any Goal" and discover more ways to work with Donna, please go to www.donnabrown.com/goals/.

15

BECAUSE I CAN

THE AWE-INSPIRING POWER OF MOMENTS THAT CHANGE EVERYTHING

"I learned how we, as humans, can support each other through tough times, for it is in seeing the silver lining, and being open to the lessons, where we can flourish – even in the most difficult situation."
– Leanne Velky

Life is a journey comprised of an infinite number of impactful moments.

Some are huge and joyous… like the day you got married, or the day you held your baby for the very first time.

Some are small and seemingly insignificant… like the time you tripped on the stairs at five years old – but you still bear a small scar on your knee to remind you that it happened.

And still, some moments rock you so deeply you're forever changed… like the day your brother died.

ALL of the moments, though, add up to making you the extraordinary human you are today.

ALL of the moments deserve their place – no matter how big or small – because each of those moments have compounded over the years to build the magnificent person you are in THIS moment.

Throughout my years growing up in Vermont, I spent a lot of time volunteering with my dad and his Rotary Club. I was always happy and eager to help out, thinking, *I want to be just like him when I grow up.*

Whether I was selling tickets to their annual fundraiser (one year I sold the most out of anyone in the club!) or joining them to volunteer for Green Up Day (a day we would go out and clean up trash from the side of the road), I always knew my heart for service was growing. Through these events, I was part of something bigger than myself. I loved seeing how I, one able-bodied and willing girl, could have a tangible impact on my community. I truly believe that being raised a Rotarian and being raised to see through a lens of love and service has helped me become a better human – a listener, a cheerleader and a proud citizen of my community.

But life isn't all butterflies and rainbows, is it? We each face hardships that bring us clearer understanding of just how incredible and fragile life is.

When I was twelve years old, while my mom and dad were away on a cruise they'd saved years to go on, my twenty-one-year-old brother fell extremely ill. He was air-vacced to Brigham &

Women's Hospital in Boston, where he lay almost lifeless for ten days.

I remember the last night I saw him. My aunt and uncle drove me to Boston where my mom and dad had been for days. We all crowded in next to my brother's bed. I stood next to the bed holding his hand, and I remember saying, "If you can hear us, squeeze my hand," and he did – ever so lightly.

I don't remember how long we were in there before we left to eat. I then settled in to a cot in the waiting room. I do remember being woken up around 1:30 a.m. by my mom rubbing my back, telling me through tears that Josh had died.

Being twelve, I didn't quite understand the enormity of this moment or how profoundly and deeply it would carry through the rest of my life.

Over time, I've come to learn that while his physical body left this world so many years ago, his spirit has always supported and guided me. He's always been my biggest cheerleader, and much of what I do and how I live my life now, is a direct result of losing my big brother so young. I'm driven by a deep fire that screams "because I can" – because he (and others) no longer can.

I was always a chipper and cheery person and I think, looking back, that much of that is because I learned so young that life is precious and fragile. That we should never utter "I hate you" to another person and we should always end the day with an "I love you."

We should seize the precious moments and once in a lifetime opportunities with loved ones. We never know when it might be the last moment we'll ever spend with someone.

When my great aunt died during my senior year of college, I immediately sunk into regret. The previous Easter, I had cancelled a trip to see her. She had planned an entire weekend of special moments for us. I can still hear her voice when I told her, ringing as clear as day, "You're kidding me! I got Broadway tickets for us." And yet, I had still decided to cancel, driving north instead of south to see her.

That has forever been one of my greatest regrets. I know that has also become a part of why I do what I do – because I see the power in shared experiences. I see the power in bringing people together for moments where we can share collectively in community… where we can speak and listen and be connected for a single moment in time… because those real moments, those real connections, are the most important things.

I want you to take a few minutes to reflect on a moment in your own life where you have felt regret. What lesson did you learn from that experience? How are you never letting the type of situation that caused the regret happen again? After my great aunt's death, I decided that I would never again take those shared moments for granted. I gained a profound understanding that life is all a series of experiences.

All of this led me to set my sights on the world of event planning after college. I wouldn't take any other job because I have a deep passion for the power of bringing people together. I believe in the power of hugs and meeting someone in real life after having only spoken to them on the phone. I also just love the hustle and bustle of events.

After months of searching, I finally landed a "dream job" at a meeting planning company. I was challenged from the moment I walked in the door to the last time I walked out. I learned more in one year there than I would have in five anywhere else (and then I gave almost five years of my life to that job). I lost sight of who I was during those years but I know I also picked up a thousand lessons and skills along the way.

I can look back now and appreciate the skills I built in writing and communications. I value learning how to compose myself under pressure and appreciate the incredible amount of energy it takes to run events.

I developed deep, meaningful and lifelong friendships with beautiful people who were going through the same experience as me. I learned how we, as humans, can support each other through tough times, for it is in seeing the silver lining, and being open to the lessons, where we can flourish – even in the most difficult situation.

In 2016, I finally "got it." I finally realized that I am an expert in my field. It suddenly felt selfish to keep my knowledge and skills tied to one single employer. So, I set out to start my own business – one that helps lots of clients and "spreads MY love" to more places. I now see so many people who are doing the same – finding that their gifts, which are often honed through struggle and trials, are what they are called to share with the world.

Entrepreneurship as a heart-centered woman has been the best adventure yet. I've grown in new and beautiful ways. Yes, this path brings those difficult moments where we could give up, throw in the towel or say we have had enough. I've had those – but then I remember that I do everything I do, because I can. It is through following our own path, leaning into the moments and creating experiences with those we serve that we can find true success in entrepreneurship – all while being true to ourselves at the same time.

Rise Up Challenge

1. Take stock of all the ways that YOU CAN. What can YOU DO, that someone close to you cannot?
2. What are the big lessons you have learned from the moments you have struggled?
3. How are you creating memories through experiences in your life and business?

About the Author

Leanne, having mastered the online event registration software Cvent during her years learning and supporting the Corporate Meetings industry, is now a successful Entrepreneur, Event Registration Expert and go-to Cvent Specialist out of Massachusetts.

Leanne has learned the ins and outs of meeting management from the ground up, including the art of crafting detailed, logistical communications. She knows what it takes to smile through the challenges and how to create a seamless customer journey that leaves a lasting impression long after an event has ended.

Keeping true to her enthusiastic, willing-to-do-anything personality, Leanne officially started her online business venture in 2016 after five years with a meeting planner and two years in Biotech. She now supports corporations and small business owners from all over, creating meaningful experiences from registration to completion for every event she's involved with.

To learn more or keep up with everything going on in Leanne's world, visit www.leannevelky.com.

16

EMBRACING IMPERFECTION

HOW RELEASING PERFECTION ALLOWED ME TO REDISCOVER HAPPINESS

"Life is not perfect. Loss, grief and personal struggles are inevitable. Our struggles are necessary, and they teach us many lessons about life, allowing us to question and improve who we are. If we don't honour the struggle, we have missed an incredible opportunity to become the highest version of ourselves."
– Jennifer Sencar

Growing up, I wanted to be the "good girl," go to school, get good grades and make my parents proud. I was always striving to be perfect. I followed the rules and from the outside it looked like I had it all, but on the inside I never felt like enough. I had a lot of friends and I was well liked, but not part of the "in" crowd. I worked hard to get excellent grades but needed a 1% higher average to get scholarships. Never being able to measure up to my own expectations made me feel like I was not enough.

Shortly after I graduated from law school, my world was rocked when my mom was diagnosed with terminal lung cancer. When she was diagnosed, we had just moved to B.C. and I was working towards completing my articles so I could start my legal career. My mom was my dad's caregiver, as he was much older and had a heart condition. My sister was only seventeen. It was too much responsibility and I was overwhelmed, but I had to keep going. I turned to exercise to cope. I wrapped my hands, put on my boxing gloves and fought my way through the intense grief and anger I felt. I punched and kicked the heavy bag until I was too exhausted to worry about the uncertainty of the future.

My mom fought her cancer for thirteen months. At age forty-eight, she died peacefully in her sleep in hospice. I was devastated, but also at peace, because her cancer journey gave me the opportunity to heal our relationship – for her to really see me. It was in those moments I spent with her while she was dying, that I realized many events in our lives are out of our control. I could only control my reaction. I chose to honour my grief, but I also chose to experience the happiness of being close to her during her last days.

Two months later, while I was still grieving the loss of my mom, my dad died. I was in shock and disbelief. My life wasn't supposed to turn out like this. I just lost my hero, my rock – the only other person who really understood and believed in me. I will never forget the day he died. It was the first time in my life that I felt truly helpless and alone. As I was watching my seventeen-year-old sister stand by his bedside, holding his hand and begging him to live, I felt numb, like I was watching the scene of a tragic movie. I thought, *Is this really happening to me? Why? What have I done to deserve this?*

As he took his last breath, I stood there, frozen. My sister fell to the floor as the grief consumed her and I began to realize I was all she had left. A wave of fear and uncertainty came over me as I realized that I was now an orphan. I was completely lost. My dad suffered throughout his lifetime with a heart condition. On his death certificate it may have said he died of congenital heart failure, but I know he died of a broken heart. He could not bear the thought of living without my mom. Again, I was reminded that I only get one life to live and any moment could be my last. I made a promise to myself that I would love and live fully.

Loss of this magnitude is profound and life altering. This loss shaped my life. I honoured all the emotions of anger, sadness and loss, but I was also able to see the beauty in the love my parents had for each other and for our family. Losing my parents left a hole in my life that I struggled with for many years. I had spent most of my life, up to that point, trying to be the perfect daughter and make them proud. I suddenly did not have a purpose anymore.

It was never in my plans to get married or have children, but I fell in love and I longed for the family I lost. I was able to get pregnant easily – however, the pregnancy and delivery were anything but perfect. I had many complications and the birth process was excruciating. It was one of the most traumatic experiences of my life. Almost everything that could go wrong, went wrong that day. I was so injured, I had to stay a long time in the hospital, and again felt lost and alone.

I loved my son more than anything, but because he was very challenging, parenting brought up a lot of difficult emotions for me. I was angry and questioned why I had decided to become a mother. He had colic, milk allergies, acid reflux, and he was overstimulated. I struggled in silence with crippling depression and guilt for not being able to care for him in the way I felt he needed. I started to lean back into the guilt of never being enough. I beat myself up and I put myself last. I was exhausted in every way, shape and form. My marriage was non-existent and I was busy keeping up appearances that everything was perfect.

I knew my son was not typical from the day he was born. However, everyone dismissed my feelings and told me he was fine. For the longest time, I felt he was my greatest failure. As it turns out, my son has ADHD, which makes him sensitive and overstimulated. I remember one time when my son was about eighteen months old… I was screaming at him in frustration and suddenly felt as though I was watching myself, looking back into my own eyes. I saw a little boy that just wanted to be understood and loved. My getting angry and yelling all the time was breaking his spirit. In that moment, I realized that I had let my fear, anxiety and perfectionism take over. I did not recognize the person I had become. I decided right then that I couldn't keep doing what I was doing. It wasn't working for me or for him. I immediately decided to drop the cloak of perfection and do it my way. I got down on the floor and looked him in the eye and instead of yelling, I decided to discipline with love.

I began taking responsibility for how I was showing up in the world. I finally decided to stop telling myself I wasn't good enough to be a mother or to have a better life. I started very simply, by focusing on love instead of judgment. I made a conscious effort to have moments of joy every day and celebrate them. We created our own love rituals after discipline. I embraced being silly with him when he needed to run off the extra energy. I chose to find happiness in at least one moment per day, even if it seemed next to impossible. These small shifts in perspective have allowed me to begin to love and accept myself for who I am, even if I am not perfect.

Although I would not have chosen to experience so much loss and grief in my life, I am grateful for the lessons and perspective they have provided me. I finally understand that my happiness is my responsibility. I have to let go of the negative stories and love myself for who I am, so I can be the happiest and healthiest version of myself.

Rise Up Challenge

We must all learn to love and appreciate more, especially in times of struggle.

1. I challenge you to stand in front of the mirror and look into your own eyes. Admire all of your imperfections.
2. Take the opportunity to appreciate yourself for three things each day and say I love you.
3. Repeat this practice every day, for thirty days, and you will drastically improve your self-love and confidence, just as I have been able to do.

About the Author

Jen Sencar is a certified success coach, speaker and wellness warrior. She has spent over a decade speaking, facilitating and training on leadership and self-development. Jen is passionate about helping women liberate themselves from burnout and stress so they can discover their true purpose.

Through her speaking and coaching programs, she motivates women to discover their gifts and tap into their true potential by learning to love themselves and creating healthy success habits.

If you would like to connect with Jen, please visit www.jennifersencar.com.

17

WE ARE WOMEN RISING

"There is no force equal to
a woman determined to rise."
- W.E.B. Dubois

Thank you for joining us on this journey of Women Rising. These stories are beautiful reminders that it is sometimes within our darkest moments, deepest doubts and greatest fears that we crack open the knowledge we have brewing within us.

The knowledge that is silenced by the noise and expectations of others.

The knowledge that is drowned in day-to-day routine.

The knowledge that we turn from because we are afraid.

Within these pages, we were invited to share in the most intimate moments of these women's lives. We held space as we heard of the loss of babies and other loved ones. As we stayed with our authors, we cheered for them as they found out how they could move forth from that loss.

We witnessed the value of both love for others and for self – and we discovered the power that love can release into our own lives. We acknowledged the importance of knowing we are enough. Each one of us. We came to understand that little voices can move big mountains, that loss and grief can force our hand, but ultimately, we choose our actions.

We came to see that time and money DO matter when it comes to happiness, that mess creates opportunity for change, that your why matters and losing sight of it can bring chaos. We pondered the sacred space between life and death that opens for an instant to teach those who need the teaching, that we are not meant to do life alone and that we have gifts and we have choice in what we do with these gifts.

We came to stand in strength, understanding we can break patterns and take a different path, that business and spirituality can merge and take you to one glorious destination, and that it is never too late to be who you dream of becoming. We saw that life gives us wake up calls and it is wise to listen to them! Going all in and being brave creates a life lived with integrity.

Dear readers, we know life is a journey comprised of an infinite number of impactful, imperfect moments that can change you forever and lead to your happiness.

Each story is part of the tapestry that defines human experience.

We seldom have a journey from start to end that is not

complicated or challenging and our task at hand now is to reflect on all we have learned and carry it forward with us. We will take these lessons and rise, because…

We Are Women Rising.

18

A MESSAGE FROM CHANTELLE ADAMS

Thank you for witnessing the unfolding of the fourth book in the Women Rising series. Every year I am humbled by the strength and resilience I see in the women who take part in this beautiful project. It always comes together just as it should, with just the right people and just the right stories. Perhaps you can see yourself taking part in a project like this? Or maybe you know you have a story to share that could change the world? Read on to learn more about what I do and how I work with people just like you. I invite you to walk alongside me on this journey to empower, clarify and support your steps forward in your life.

It is an honour to be the connector who brings all these women together to share their stories in this collaborative book series, Women Rising. It is my calling to help others see how their life experience leads to their life's work. The power of story allows us to connect to the rich meaning woven throughout our own unique path. I love showing each woman how to find clarity in her message, confidence in her voice, and the platform to share her story.

But, what is the big picture meaning behind my calling to do this work? That we need more women's voices being shared and heard. We need to find our truth and SPEAK it boldly for all to hear, so that together we can create a ripple effect of change in the world. The world will be healed as women speak up and share their message. We need more women to claim big stages and shine bright because through their words, they will change lives.

Are you interested in finding your voice, owning your story and sharing it in a bigger way? Connect with me and I can help! Here are some ways I can support you on your journey to the stage:

Centre Stage Online VIP Experience
My MISSION: To help authors, entrepreneurs and change-makers harness the power of their story while creating a standing ovation worthy speech that gets booked. I believe we can turn

these messages into a movement that creates massive positive change in the world.

This is NOT just another online program. It is a full on 1:1 experience in a group format, PLUS... a LIVE, two day in-person workshop... *Command the Stage* immersive program... tons of support + prizes!

Want to know more about the experience? Check out all the details and join us for the next round (or sign up for the wait list once the next round is full) at www.joincentrestage.com.

Centre Stage Live Event
I have worked with women from all over the world, helping them to write standing ovation worthy speeches and gain the confidence they need to speak and share their message on the stage.

The knowledge I share comes from direct experience: I have personally delivered over 800 speeches in the last five years. I have been able to add six figures to my income through speaking while spreading my message.

Are you SO ready to do the same? Are you destined to share your message in a BIG way? Are you willing to take that TED stage (or any stage for that matter) by storm? Speaking is a vehicle that can take you where you want to go. Skyrocket your name to fame while making a HUGE positive impact in the world!

No more waiting. YOU are why I created an extraordinary one-of-a-kind live event that gives you everything you need to make your speaking career happen NOW.

The *Centre Stage Live VIP Event* will give you clarity on your message and story. You'll work with me 1:1, craft your TED-style speech and speak LIVE on stage. In addition, you will receive a professional demo video; you'll be treated like a celebrity with hair, makeup and styling; you'll have three different photo shoots... Top this off by enjoying your stay at the GORGEOUS five diamond resort, Sparkling Hills.

You get everything you need to get booked and PAID to SPEAK (walking away with your demo video, speaker one-sheet design, testimonials and so much more) while gaining the CONFIDENCE to share your message in a massive way! Not only do you get ALL of this amazingness at a MASSIVE value, you will also get a chance to SPEAK on the highly coveted stage at *Shine Live* – my three day event for powerhouse, change-making women!

If you are ready to change your life and the lives of others through the power of your voice, join *Centre Stage Live*. Learn how to sign up at www.chantelleadams.com/centre-stage-live/.

Shine Live

Imagine an event filled with 150+ powerful, change-making women who are stepping into their confidence and having the courage to share their voice with the world in a BIG way. They are ready to shine their light and you know you belong with them. You will be seen, heard and celebrated!

You will be part of a collaborative movement where women entrepreneurs are truly SHINING a light on who they are. You'll find your bigger mission and purpose while changing the world with your voice.

Find details on the next *Shine Live* event at www.shinelive.chantelleadams.com.

FREE Workbook: 21 Ways to Get Booked to Speak
Get FREE access! *21 Ways to Get Booked to Speak* shares all of my BEST strategies. These guidelines helped me get booked over 800 times in five years, averaging about 175 speaking gigs a year (90% of which were paid gigs). If you follow even just a few of these strategies, you will be getting booked to speak in no time. Get the guide at www.chantelleadams.com/getbooked/.

ABOUT WOMEN RISING SERIES

The ***Women Rising Series*** is the brainchild of Chantelle Adams. All four books are available on Amazon. The last two of them are also available for Kindle.

If you enjoy the stories and believe in the importance of Women Rising, please consider leaving a book review on Amazon. Thank you in advance for supporting this vision.

Made in the USA
Middletown, DE
06 December 2018